DEAR PR*SIDENT A**CLOWN:
101 MORE RUDE LETTERS
TO DONALD TRUMP

Copyright © 2019 Aldous J. Pennyfarthing

All rights reserved

Published by:
Pennyfarthing & Dash Publishing, a wholly owned subsidiary of O'Reilly's Falafels and Loofahs Inc.

ALDOUS J. PENNYFARTHING

Aldous J. Pennyfarthing lives in the Pacific Northwest with his beloved wife, Penelope Middleton-Smythe, and their mutt terrier, Fiddlehead Stinktrousers.

In contrast to Donald Trump's shambolic bearing, appearance, and comportment, Pennyfarthing is a natty hail-fellow-well-met and a gentleman. He resorts to the fatuous japery contained in this book out of a sincere love for country.

Also by Aldous J. Pennyfarthing:

*Dear F*cking Lunatic: 101 Obscenely Rude Letters to Donald Trump*

*Dear F*cking Moron: 101 More Rude Letters to Donald Trump*

The Fierce, Fabulous (and Mostly Fictional) Adventures of Mike Ponce, America's First Gay Vice President

Also, follow my posts at Daily Kos, and be sure to sign up!

And check out my Facebook page at Facebook.com/trumpworstpresident and my Twitter @AJPennyfarthing.

Special thanks to Ms. Emma Dash for the help and encouragement — and for loaning me a heaping cup of insults.

Oh, sinnerman, where you gonna run to?
Sinnerman where you gonna run to?
Where you gonna run to?
All on that day

INTRODUCTION

Jesus Christ, this asshole.

Seriously.

Many years ago, before Donald Trump the presidential candidate started spraying his mind diarrhea all over our collective Jungian unconscious, I was a callow, Pollyannish political junkie who could still confect a precise measure of mirth and outrage over the fact that Dan Quayle couldn't spell "potato."

There I would stand — a dry Belvedere martini in my right hand, an opera-length cigarette holder balanced between the delicate, tapered, alabaster fingers of my left — as I skewered the know-nothing philistines across the aisle with my surpassing Voltairean wit.

"Oh, *heavens*," I tittered, regaling my upper east side Manitowoc* society friends with a dazzling volley of urbane flourishes. "Dan Quayle can't spell *potato*. Can you imagine? I mean, what's next? Ho, ho, ho, ho, ho!"

Needless to say, I want to go back in time to meet 1992 Aldous so I can preemptively beat him to death with a remaindered copy of *The Art of the Deal*. Because I would Gorilla Glue my balls to a Mackinac Island taffy-pulling machine if it meant Dan Quayle could be president right now, and that can't happen as long as this timeline remains intact. Who knows? My praising

Dan Quayle to the rafters back in the early '90s could be all we need to derail this ayahuasca fart of a reality and get back to something resembling normalcy.

You see, once upon a time we lived in a world where something like — I don't know — a credible rape accusation against a sitting president was earth-shattering enough to stop the whole of Christendom in its tracks.

Today, unless "45th president and multiply accused alleged rapist" shows up as a crossword puzzle clue, the story is out of the newspapers in less than a week.

On June 21, 2019, *New York* magazine ran a book excerpt from veteran journalist E. Jean Carroll in which she claimed Donald Trump had raped her in a department store dressing room.

The story jibed with everything we know about Trump, and yet it disappeared from the headlines faster than a passed-out hooker from a Mar-a-Lago cabana.

In denying the accusation, Trump attacked Carroll's looks as subtly as a Trump can: "Number one, she's not my type. Number two, it never happened. It never happened, okay?"

Uh huh. So Trump is really choosy about the women he rapes? Is that what he's trying to say? And what's with the snide allusion to her appearance?

First of all, Donald Trump looks like 12 different kinds of scrotum patched together with gently used dental floss and gum. So he really shouldn't be making *any* sort of comment on another human being's appearance.

Secondly, rape has nothing to do with physical attraction. It's about dominance and humiliation — which we all know are Donald Trump's stock-in-trade.

Finally, the only sensible way to approach a Donald Trump statement is to assume it's false unless you have *extremely* compelling evidence to the contrary. The guy lies as often as he exhales. Hence, Carroll's story easily cleared the threshold for credible accusations.

So did it stick?

Nah.

The media spilled a soupçon of ink over the he-said/she-said back-and-forth and then quickly moved on to the next barrel of salty filberts.

And can you blame them? There's just too much outrage, shit-slurping insanity, and rank dishonesty to get a handle on in this transcendently outrageous, insane, and dishonest era.

So I had to start writing these letters to Donald Trump — our illustrious asshole-in-chief — to 1) keep myself sane, 2) provide a needed catharsis to my kindred spirits (i.e., all y'all), and 3) see if I can somehow bore through Trump's cranium to the rich nougat center inside and plant a seed of sanity therein.

1) is accomplished. I sure hope 2) is happening. 3) is a long, long slog currently in progress. (Does anyone have a diamond drill bit they could lend me?)

But these books — and you can find the first two installments, *Dear F*cking Lunatic* and *Dear F*cking Moron*, at a website near new you — are not just Hail Mary attempts at an intervention. They also serve as a chronicle. The sheer volume of Trump scandals, Trump gaffes, and Trump stupidity is simply overwhelming. My sincere hope is to gather in the boom harvest of wanton fucknuttery from the Trump years and try to scrape together a few crusts of bread with which to nourish and salve our weary souls.

So here we go again.

If this is your intro to Pennyfarthing, I urge you to go back and read the first two installments in this series. You'll find a complete primer on Pennyfarthing therein.

Incidentally, the working title for my next — and what I pray to all that is good and holy will be my last — installment in this tetralogy is *Goodbye, Asshole*.

Please make that one the last in the series. Please. Only you, the long-tormented members of our country's sane community, can make it so. I need — we *all* need — the rest.

Thank you.

And enjoy.

*Yes, I was born and raised in Manitowoc, Wisconsin. No, I don't know Steven Avery. Stop fucking asking.

April 1, 2019

- Trump tweets, "Everybody agrees that ObamaCare doesn't work. Premiums & deductibles are far too high - Really bad HealthCare! Even the Dems want to replace it, but with Medicare for all, which would cause 180 million Americans to lose their beloved private health insurance. The Republicans are developing a really great HealthCare Plan with far lower premiums (cost) & deductibles than ObamaCare. In other words it will be far less expensive & much more usable than ObamaCare. Vote will be taken right after the Election when Republicans hold the Senate & win back the House. It will be truly great HealthCare that will work for America. Also, Republicans will always support Pre-Existing Conditions. The Republican Party will be known as the Party of Great Healt-Care [sic]. Meantime, the USA is doing better than ever & is respected again!"

From the Desk of Aldous J. Pennyfarthing
To: Donald Trump, our long national nightmare

Dear Pr*sident Assclown,

Wait, how the fuck can you be getting *crazier*? I mean, what's the endgame? If you dissolved into a colony of fruit bats and blotted out the sun for a fortnight, causing global harvest failures and touching off a 100-year world war between the U.S. and a subterranean race of gonorrheal she-orcs, I'd be, like, "Huh. Yeah. That sounds about right."

I swear, every day you're pr*sident feels like drowning in a sperm whale's vagina with a crate of unexploded Korean War ordnance lodged up my ass.

For the love of God, shut your fucking trap already. Your mouth is the size of a bulimic gerbil's asshole and yet every single day ushers in another Mount St. Helens eruption of arabesque bullshit.

Fuuuuuuuuccccccccckkkkkk me sideways with Milton Berle's legendary showbiz schlong. I can't take much more.

You're the one who's allegedly president. So why the fuck are *we* stressed out 24/7?

Maybe I'd like to go golfing occasionally, too — but I live in transcendent terror, relentlessly haunted by the metaphysical certainty that the nuclear football will eventually be left behind at a Tijuana donkey show.

Have you read *any* of my previous correspondence? Please, I'm not doing this for my "Healt." If I wanted to improve my "Healt" I'd move to fucking Canada and drink Carling Black Label until I collapsed face-first into an ice-fishing hole. Because, you know, universal "Healt" care.

Please stop freaking us the fuck out, Ty-orangesaurus rectum.

We have less than two years left of this shit. Try not to blow us all up, okay?

Love,
Pennyfarthing

❖ ❖ ❖

April 2, 2019

- Trump tweets, "The best thing that ever happened to Puerto Rico is President Donald J. Trump. So many wonderful people, but with such bad Island leadership and with so much money wasted. Cannot continue to hurt our Farmers and States with these massive payments, and so little appreciation!"
- While discussing Trump's offensive and inaccurate tweets about Puerto Rico, Trump spokesperson Hogan Gidley refers to the U.S. territory as "that country."
- Speaking to reporters about the Mueller report, Trump says, "I hope they now go and take a look at the oranges. The oranges of the, uh, uh, investigation." He also claims his father, who was born in New York, was actually born in Germany. He *further* claims that he'll be releasing a health care plan that's "much better than Obamacare" if Republicans take back the House in 2020.
- At a Republican fundraising event, Trump says, "If you have a windmill anywhere near your house, congratulations: Your house just went down 75 percent in value. And they say the noise causes cancer. You tell me that one, okay."

From the Desk of Aldous J. Pennyfarthing
To: Donald Trump, witless cocksplat

Dear Pr*sident Assclown,

So you shot way the fuck past "vaccines cause autism" and landed squarely on windmill cancer. Listen, I know pants-shitting crazy is your bailiwick, but here's some advice: You're supposed to go bonkers in increments. It's way more interesting that way. What if Jack Nicholson had chased Shelley Duvall around with an ax the minute they checked into the Overlook Hotel? Totally different fucking movie, dude. And pretty boring.

So ... "they say the noise causes cancer." Who's the "they" in that sentence? Did you have Michele Bachmann's and Randy Quaid's consciousness uploaded into your brain at some secret government facility in Area 51? Because that sounds more fun than drugs. Must be nice to be pr*sident.

Also, you keep bragging about how much better and cost-efficient your (by all accounts nonexistent) health care plan is than Obama's. Let me guess. Because it covers windmill cancer. And since that doesn't exist, the premiums are really, really reasonable.

Oh, and don't think that just because you raised the frightening specter of windmill cancer on the same day that you demanded we get to the bottom of the "oranges" of the Mueller investigation that we're going to just overlook *that* gem, Jiminy Citrus.

You really need to get the folds of your brain checked for lint and paperclips and Tic Tacs and shit. There might even be a few loose quarters in there. I'm guessing your cranium looks like the inside of a frat house couch following a baker's dozen or so robust masturbation sessions.

In other words, GET HELP!

Jesus.

Love,

Pennyfarthing

April 3, 2019

- House Ways and Means Committee Chair Richard Neal asks the IRS for six years of Trump's tax returns.
- Trump tweets, "I was never planning a vote prior to the 2020 Election on the wonderful HealthCare package that some very talented people are now developing for me & the Republican Party. It will be on full display during the Election as a much better & less expensive alternative to ObamaCare…"

April 4, 2019

- Speaking with reporters, Trump says, "We're going to give them a one-year warning, and if the drugs don't stop or (are) largely stopped, we're going to put tariffs on Mexico and products, in particular, the cars … and if that doesn't stop the drugs, we close the border."
- Trump says he's recommending former presidential candidate and fellow sexual harassment accusee Herman Cain for a seat on the Federal Reserve Board.

April 5, 2019

- Trump tweets, "The press is doing everything within their power to fight the magnificence of the phrase, MAKE AMERICA GREAT AGAIN! They can't stand the fact that this Administration has done more than virtually any other Administration in its first 2yrs. They are truly the ENEMY OF THE PEOPLE!"

April 7, 2019

- DHS Secretary Kirstjen Nielsen resigns.
- Acting White House chief of staff Mick Mulvaney says Democrats will never see Trump's tax returns.

April 8, 2019

- Several media outlets report that Secret Service director Randolph "Tex" Alles is being removed from his post per Trump's request. *The New York Times* reports that Trump made fun of Alles, calling him "Dumbo" because his ears stuck out.
- NBC News reports that Trump "for months" lobbied for the reinstatement of family separation at the border as a way to deter asylum-seekers. DHS Secretary Kirstjen Nielsen reportedly resisted his calls for a return to the policy.

April 9, 2019

- CNN reports that Trump told aides he was putting senior policy adviser Stephen Miller in charge of all immigration and border issues. The network also reports that Trump wanted former DHS Secretary Kirstjen Nielsen to get tougher on illegal border crossings, including by deterring migrants through family separations. "He just wants to separate families," a senior administration official told the network.

From the Desk of Aldous J. Pennyfarthing
To: Donald Trump, Cheeto-faced flesh bag

Dear Pr*sident Assclown,

"He just wants to separate families" is such an awful, execrable, inhuman, Brobdingnagian shit mound of a sentence, I'm surprised it's not your campaign slogan. Maybe trial-balloon it on a T-shirt or something. I'm sure China would give you a good price on them. No doubt you can find some way around our idiotic tariffs.

And you're putting Stephen Fucking Miller in charge of immigration? Stephen Miller is what you'd get if you gypsy-cursed Heinrich Himmler's soul into Eva Braun's dildo. If you put all the evil in the world in a centrifuge with a flask of curdled mole rat semen, you could create an army of Stephen Millers. Though I can only assume they'd all show up to boot camp with notes from their doctors saying they can't participate, and then what are you left with? An army of racist twats endlessly chafing their unnaturally spawned dinguses.

So I guess this is as good a time as any to bring up this story, from Vox:

> The Trump administration rejected a study conducted by its own Department of Health and Human Services finding that refugees had a net positive value in the United States over the past decade, according to a recent report by the New York Times.
>
> The study found that between 2005 and 2014, refugees "contributed an estimated $269.1 billion in revenues to all levels of government" through the payment of federal, state, and local taxes — which far outweighed their cost to the country. "Overall, this report estimated that the net fiscal impact of

refugees was positive over the 10-year period, at $63 billion." When the study was completed in July, however, it was never publicly released, and the Trump administration dismissed the findings.

So immigrants as a whole contributed $63 billion more than they cost the government in a decade. Meanwhile, you once *lost* $1 billion over the course of a decade — which prevented you from paying *any* taxes for several years.

So if we based federal policy on reality instead of unvarnished racism, we'd have to deport *you*.

One can dream, right?

Love,
Pennyfarthing

◆ ◆ ◆

April 10, 2019

- Trump tweets, "So, it has now been determined, by 18 people that truly hate President Trump, that there was No Collusion with Russia. In fact, it was an illegal investigation that should never have been allowed to start. I fought back hard against this Phony & Treasonous Hoax!"

April 12, 2019

- Trump says he's "giving strong consideration" to sending immigrants who cross the border to sanctuary cities, apparently as a way to spite those cities.

April 13, 2019

- Trump tweets, "When I won the Election in 2016, the @nytimes had to beg their fleeing subscribers for forgiveness in that they covered the Election (and me) so badly. They didn't have a clue, it was pathetic. They even apologized to me. But now they are even worse, really corrupt reporting!"
- During an interview on a Christian radio program, former congresswoman and presidential candidate Michele Bachmann says Trump "is highly biblical, and I would say to your listeners, we will in all likelihood never see a more godly, biblical president again in our lifetime."

From the Desk of Aldous J. Pennyfarthing
To: Donald Trump, preying man-tits

Dear Pr*sident Assclown,

- Lust
- Gluttony
- Greed
- Sloth
- Wrath
- Envy
- Pride

Sorry. It's the weekend. I was finishing my Sunday to-do list. This has nothing to do with you. Nothing at all. Oh, no. Far from it.

But while we're on the subject, you *are* the apotheosis of the Seven Deadly Sins. And you know this, right? I mean, it couldn't be any clearer.

Granted, Michele Bachmann is about three dead brain cells away from thinking she's a Keebler elf, but I remain gobsmacked that fundie Christians as a whole are so in thrall to the demonstrably *least* Christ-like man in Washington.

Remember when Jesus said, "Suffer the little children to come unto me, so I can arrest them, tear them away from their desperate immigrant parents, lock them in cages, and who gives a righteous flying fuck if they have cancer"? No? Me neither.

And let's be honest. You've spent more time inside porn stars than churches. And I'd wager it's not even close.

So what's your secret? Because I might want to grift some hateful rubes, too.

What does Michele Bachmann see that I don't see — other than green absinthe fairies and tiny goblins rowing around on spearmint gum wrappers in her Applebee's chicken tortilla soup?

Love,
Pennyfarthing

April 15, 2019

- Trump tweets, "What do I know about branding, maybe nothing (but I did become President!), but if I were Boeing, I would FIX the Boeing 737 MAX, add some additional great features, & REBRAND the plane with a new name. No product has suffered like this one. But again, what the hell do I know?"
- After a fire threatens Notre Dame Cathedral, Trump tweets, "So horrible to watch the massive fire at Notre Dame Cathedral in Paris. Perhaps flying water tankers could be used to put it out. Must act quickly!"

From the Desk of Aldous J. Pennyfarthing
To: Donald Trump, flaccid shitgoblin

Dear Pr*sident Assclown,

So, got any other advice? You appear to have plenty of time on your hands.

Why don't you pop on over to MIT and heckle a few superstring theorists?

But it's always good to remind firefighters who are *at that very moment* busy fighting fires that they "must act quickly." Oh, and that water might somehow be productively leveraged toward the extinguishing of said fires. Before you tweeted, they were gripped with ennui and existential malaise as they languidly beat the Notre Dame Cathedral fire to death with their poncy coxcomb wigs.

You saved the Notre Dame Cathedral! Sweet! Imagine how focking proud you'd be if you'd known it existed yesterday!

Still, not everyone was so keen on your kibitzing. For instance, the French Interior Ministry's Civil Security and Crisis Management agency later tweeted, "All means are being used, except for water-bombing aircrafts which, if used, could lead to the collapse of the entire structure of the cathedral."

Wait, that sounds like they used literally every means at their disposal to extinguish the fire *except* for the stupid thing you said.

But hold on a second! You saw water-bombing planes on the teevee once! That has to mean something, or else what has your life been all about?

Stick to what you know, which as far as I can tell is pretty much limited to cheating at golf, spray-tanning your head until it looks like a Costco rotisserie chicken, and panic-shoveling quicklime onto dead hookers.

Love,

Pennyfarthing

April 16, 2019

- Attorney General William Barr orders judges to deny bail to asylum seekers waiting for their cases to be heard.
- Trump vetoes a bipartisan resolution calling for the end of U.S. involvement in Yemen's civil war.
- Trump tweets, "I believe it will be Crazy Bernie Sanders vs. Sleepy Joe Biden as the two finalists to run against maybe the best Economy in the history of our Country (and MANY other great things)! I look forward to facing whoever it may be. May God Rest Their Soul!"

April 18, 2019

- The redacted version of the Mueller report is released. Trump tweets a *Game of Thrones*-inspired image that says, "No Collusion. No Obstruction. For the haters and the radical left Democrats — Game Over."
- A footnote from the redacted Mueller report says Trump could be exposed to criminal prosecution once he's out of office: "A Sitting President's Amenability to Indictment and Criminal Prosecution, 24 Op. O.L.C. at 255 ('Recognizing an immunity from prosecution for a sitting President would not preclude such prosecution once the President's term is over or he is otherwise removed from office by resignation or impeachment.')."

April 19, 2019

- Despite having (falsely) claimed that the Mueller report proves he and his campaign engaged in "no collusion" and "no obstruction," Trump tweets that the report was "crazy": "Statements are made about me by certain people in the Crazy Mueller Report, in itself written by 18 Angry Democrat Trump Haters, which are fabricated & totally untrue. Watch out for people that take so-called 'notes,' when the notes never existed until needed. Because I never agreed to testify, it was not necessary for me to respond to statements made in the 'Report' about me, some of which are total bullshit & only given to make the other person look good (or me to look bad). This was an Illegally Started Hoax that never should have happened."

April 21, 2019

- Trump tweets, "Happy Easter! I have never been happier or more content because your Country is doing so well, with an Economy that is the talk of the World and may be stronger than it has ever been before. Have a great day!"

From the Desk of Aldous J. Pennyfarthing
To: Donald Trump, weapons-grade knob

Dear Pr*sident Assclown,

Jesus is risen! And so am I! Praise me as I sit upon my magnificent golden throne shitting luminous celestial turds and taking credit for Barack Obama's accomplishments!

I was so hopeful when my eyes first lit upon your tweet because I noticed that you correctly capitalized the first two words. I thought, "Oh, my. Will my president show a moment of lucidity and humility at last? And he said 'Happy Easter,' not 'Happy Easter to all the losers and haters'! He's evolving!"

But no. The most important day on the Christian calendar has nothing to do with the saving grace of Christ. It's all about our unnecessarily capitalized Economy and the guy who thinks he deserves credit for it.

Again, Barack Obama turned the economy around and you're simply coasting on that runaway toboggan right into the nearest tree. We can all see it. It's coming. Break out the hot apple cider and leg splints.

I won't mention that job creation has actually slowed down significantly since you became president, or that the S&P 500 went up far more during Barack Obama's first two years than during the same period of your presidency. Because I need the space for more insults about your giant adobe mud hut of a head.

But, yeah, you're just along for the ride, my friend. Enjoy it while you can before God notices and scrapes you off the bottom of His shoe like the stray shred of toilet paper you are.

Love,
Pennyfarthing

❖ ❖ ❖

April 22, 2019

- Columbia University constitutional scholar Philip Bobbitt tells *The Washington Post* that the Mueller report is "an invitation to impeachment. It certainly does not count the other way: It's not a report that closes the book on impeachment."

April 23, 2019

- Trump's Treasury Department misses a second congressional deadline for handing over Trump's tax returns.
- Trump tweets, "The Wall is being rapidly built! The Economy is GREAT! Our Country is Respected again!"
- Jared Kushner says the Mueller investigation was more harmful to the country than Russian election interference itself, which amounted to "some Facebook ads."

From the Desk of Aldous J. Pennyfarthing
To: Donald Trump, gold pricker

Dear Pr*sident Assclown,

Why do you let Jared Kushner talk? In the Dipshit Olympics, you're Usain Bolt and he's wandering around Olympic Village trying to figure out how to sign up for synchronized chub-flogging.

No, Russian election interference didn't amount to "some Facebook ads." According to the Mueller report, "[t]he Russian government interfered in the 2016 presidential election in sweeping and systematic fashion."

Oh, and there's more!

> As set forth in detail in this report, the Special Counsel's investigation established that Russia interfered in the 2016 presidential election principally through two operations. First, a Russian entity carried out a social media campaign that favored presidential candidate Donald J. Trump and disparaged presidential candidate Hillary Clinton. Second, a Russian intelligence service conducted computer-intrusion operations against entities, employees, and volunteers working on the Clinton Campaign and

then released stolen documents. The investigation also identified numerous links between the Russian government and the Trump Campaign. Although the investigation established that the Russian government perceived it would benefit from a Trump presidency and worked to secure that outcome, and that the Campaign expected it would benefit electorally from information stolen and released through Russian efforts, the investigation did not establish that members of the Trump Campaign conspired or coordinated with the Russian government in its election interference activities.

In other words, your campaign knew perfectly well what Russia was up to and didn't alert the FBI. That sorta makes you a — what's the word? —feculent, cocknosed, scurfy, twatfaced, fusty-dead-nanny-moldering-in-an-air-duct, piss-flapping, shart-huffing, dick-whistling, languorous, flayed taint of a traitor.

Okay, that's at least 14 words. To be fair.

Love,
Pennyfarthing

❖ ❖ ❖

April 24, 2019

- Trump tells reporters, "We have been, I have been the most transparent president and administration in the history of our country by far."

From the Desk of Aldous J. Pennyfarthing
To: Donald Trump, the invisible Klansman

Dear Pr*sident Assclown,

"We have been, I have been the most transparent president and administration in the history of our country by far" ... says the guy who knows releasing his tax returns would make him less popular than Jared from Subway.

Also, the Mueller report proved that you're nothing if not a criminal obstructer. You threw up dozens of roadblocks while that investigation was happening. The world hasn't seen obstruction like that since I vomit-choked myself into a mild coma on the night of your election.

Believe me, no one wants a transparent version of you. It would be less welcome than Crystal Pepsi and head cheese. That said, it would be nice if you apologized for just *one* of the 10,000 lies — and counting — you've told since becoming pr*sident.

You can start with "I have been the most transparent president ... in the history of our country by far."

Dude. Jimmy Carter felt guilty about lusting in his heart for women other than his wife and was compelled to tell the world about it, even though ***checks notes*** ... oh, here it is ... EVERYONE lusts in their heart for other people.

Meanwhile, you bang porn stars with your pertinaciously fungal bog crotch and lie your ass off about it.

So, no. I'm not buying this.

And neither is anyone else.

Also ***checks notes*** eat a dick, you off-brand peep-show squeegee.

Love,
Pennyfarthing

April 25, 2019

- The Trump campaign sends out an "Official Obama-Russia Accountability Survey" that includes questions such as "Do you believe Obama doing nothing gave Russians the green light to interfere in the 2016 Election?" and "Do you believe Obama did nothing so that Russians would help him with his Disastrous Iranian Nuclear Deal?"
- In an interview with Sean Hannity, Trump admits his accusation that Barack Obama wiretapped his office in Trump Tower was based on no real evidence: "I don't know if you remember, a long time ago, very early on I used the word wiretap, and I put in quotes, meaning surveillance — spying, you can sort of say whatever you want. Now I understand why, because they thought two years ago when I said that just on a little bit of a hunch and a little bit of wisdom maybe, it blew up because they thought maybe I was wise to them."

April 26, 2019

- To the delight of the NRA, Trump announces that he'll pull out of an international treaty intended to regulate the conventional arms industry.
- Trump, whose go-to catchphrase for 12 years on *The Apprentice* was "you're fired," claims he never tried to fire special counsel Robert Mueller because firing people is "not good": "I'm a student of history. I see what you get when you fire people and it is not good. But there would have been nothing wrong with firing him. Legally, I had absolute right to fire, but I never told Don McGahn to fire Mueller."

April 27, 2019

- At a rally in Green Bay, Wisconsin, Trump says, "100,000 illegal immigrants arrived in our borders, placing a massive strain on communities and schools and hospitals and public resources like nobody's ever seen before. Now we're sending many of them to sanctuary cities. I'm proud to tell you that was my sick idea."
- Trump tweets congratulations to Nick Bosa, the second overall pick in the NFL draft, rather than Heisman Trophy winner and first overall pick Kyler Murray. Bosa is white and Murray is black.

From the Desk of Aldous J. Pennyfarthing
To: Donald Trump, bloviating hatewanker

Dear Pr*sident Assclown,

Let's see, are you congratulating the second-place person because you got 3 million fewer votes than your 2016 opponent and still "won" or because the first-place person is, uh, black?

Well done, Barge Schott. I guess you're not even trying to hide it anymore, huh?

Of course, after "shithole countries," birtherism, the Central Park Five, housing discrimination, Frederick Douglass, "look at my African-American over here," and dozens of other wackadoodle "racially tinged" incidents, what's the point, really?

Then again, I *thought* I once heard you say, "I am the least racist person you'll ever meet." I mean, that can't be right, can it? Sure, I've been a little hard of hearing ever since that time your Charlottesville speech gave me ear syphilis, but still.

Maybe you actually said, "I am a yeast-based person who severs beets." Because while that's inscrutably Dadaistic, at least it's marginally plausible.

"I am a beast-faced person with leather sheets?"

Literally *anything* makes more sense than what I *thought* you said.

So, yeah, *go white guy!* It's so tough for a white man in today's world.

Wait a second. I just thought of another possibility. Are you congratulating him because the black guy got drafted in his place? Well, shoot. And he didn't even have to fake bone spurs.

Yeah, that's gotta be it.

Congrats to you, Obergropenführer.

Love,
Pennyfarthing

April 28, 2019

- *The Washington Post* reports that Trump doesn't like Secretary of Education Betsy DeVos, but "the president shows no signs of asking her to resign, reflecting in part his lack of interest in the issue of education and the department responsible for it."

April 29, 2019

- Deputy Attorney General Rod Rosenstein announces his resignation.
- Trump serves fast food at the White House to the national champion Baylor women's basketball team.

April 30, 2019

- *The Washington Post* reports that undocumented workers at the Trump National Golf Club Westchester in Briarcliff Manor, New York, were forced to do "side work" without pay.
- Fifty-five percent of respondents in an ABC News/*Washington Post* poll say they "definitely would not" vote for Trump in 2020.

May 1, 2019

- The Senate Judiciary Committee questions Attorney General William Barr over his handling of the Mueller report. Barr insists that he handled the report properly.

May 2, 2019

- Trump pulls the plug on crank economist Stephen Moore's nomination to the Federal Reserve Board. Moore had once admitted, "Well, you know, I'm not an expert on monetary policy."
- The Trump administration rolls back offshore-drilling regulations put in place following the 2010 Deepwater Horizon oil spill.
- During a National Day of Prayer service, Trump says he got through the Mueller investigation by leaning on his supposed faith: "People say, 'How do you get through that whole stuff? How do you go through those witch hunts and everything else?' We just do it, right. And we think about God."

From the Desk of Aldous J. Pennyfarthing
To: Donald Trump, God's totally-not-funny practical joke

Dear Pr*sident Assclown,

I really want to know how often you think about God as opposed to, say, nougat. Because I think nougat wins. Just a hunch.

Also, inviting you to a National Day of Prayer service is like asking the pope to give a solemn invocation while I languidly jerk off to anime characters on a Knight Rider beanbag chair. It makes no sense, in other words. Because you're as religious as a sautéed pelican shart and everyone knows it.

And for the last time, the Mueller investigation wasn't a witch hunt. Okay? You didn't think about God during the investigation. You thought about Bill Barr and all the Bill Barr-y things he was going to do to make you look innocent, even though you were so far up Putin's ass you needed a snorkel.

By the way, here was my favorite bit from the Mueller report: "If we had confidence after a thorough investigation of the facts that the President clearly did not commit obstruction of justice, we would so state."

In other words, you were let off the hook because of a DOJ policy that says you can't charge a sitting president.

So shut the fuck up about God already. You wouldn't know God if She punched you in the dick.

Love,
Pennyfarthing

May 3, 2019

- Trump tweets, "The wonderful Diamond and Silk

- have been treated so horribly by Facebook. They work so hard and what has been done to them is very sad - and we're looking into. It's getting worse and worse for Conservatives on social media!"
- Following an hour-long phone call between Trump and Vladimir Putin in which Trump failed to challenge Putin on election meddling, former FBI Assistant Director for Counterintelligence Frank Figliuzzi says Trump has given Russian a "green light" to attack us again.

May 4, 2019

- North Korea fires several projectiles off its east coast, including what many experts believe was a short-range ballistic missile.
- Trump retweets the alt-right account Deep State Exposed, which traffics in weird conspiracy theories, including QAnon.

May 5, 2019

- Trump tweet-whines that two years of his presidency have been "stollen": "Despite the tremendous success that I have had as President, including perhaps the greatest ECONOMY and most successful first two years of any President in history, they have stollen [sic] two years of my (our) Presidency (Collusion Delusion) that we will never be able to get back."
- Trump tweets, "The Kentuky [sic] Derby decision was not a good one. It was a rough and tumble race on a wet and sloppy track, actually, a beautiful thing

to watch. Only in these days of political correctness   occur. The best horse did NOT   rby - not even close!"

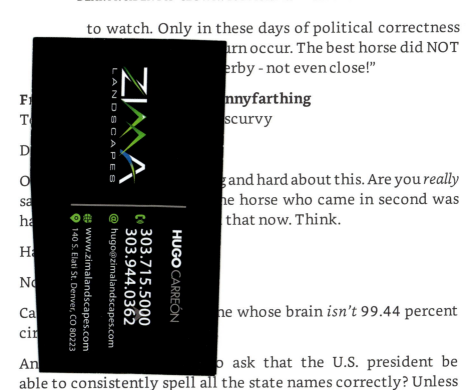

Fr   nnyfarthing
To   scurvy

D

O   and hard about this. Are you *really*
sa   he horse who came in second was
ha   that now. Think.

Ha

No

Ca   he whose brain *isn't* 99.44 percent
cir

An   o ask that the U.S. president be able to consistently spell all the state names correctly? Unless "Kentuky Derby" is a knock-off Chinese horsemeat brand, you spelled that wrong.

Then again, if you were any further to the left of the IQ bell curve they'd be forced to hose you down once a fortnight like livestock.

You *still* don't get it, do you?

Okay, let's move on.

Love,
Pennyfarthing

May 6, 2019

- Trump awards the Presidential Medal of Freedom to

- fellow adulterer and golfer Tiger Woods.
- Hundreds of former federal prosecutors sign a statement saying Trump would have been charged with obstruction based on the findings in the Mueller report were he not president.

May 7, 2019

- *The New York Times* reports that Trump lost more money from 1985 to 1994 (i.e., more than $1 billion) than any other U.S. taxpayer.

From the Desk of Aldous J. Pennyfarthing
To: Donald Trump, soggy assbag

Dear Pr*sident Assclown,

Uh, I'm not an MBA or anything, but from what I understand, a businessman losing a billion dollars is a little like a zoo director getting kidnapped and viciously pink-bellied by squirrel monkeys. And yet millions of people still think you're the best at what you do. And that's true, I guess, since "what you do" appears to be losing as much of your creditors' money as possible.

But, hey, you did call yourself the King of Debt before the election. And still nearly half the people who voted in 2016 pulled the lever for *you*. How can that be? I mean, you don't go to a prostitute whose Craigslist ad says she's the Queen of Hepatitis B, do you?

Well, most people don't. I assume you'd fuck a blobfish if she came with a free bowl of soup.

Here's my favorite bit from *The New York Times*' story on this:

> At his nadir, in the post-recession autumn of 1991, Mr. Trump testified before a congressional task force,

calling for changes in the tax code to benefit his industry.

"The real estate business — we're in an absolute depression," Mr. Trump told the lawmakers, adding: "I see no sign of any kind of upturn at all. There is no incentive to invest. Everyone is doing badly, everyone."

Everyone, perhaps, except his father, Fred Trump.

While Donald Trump reported hundreds of millions of dollars in losses for 1990 and 1991, Fred Trump's returns showed a positive income of $53.9 million, with only one major loss: $15 million invested in his son's latest apartment project.

Oh, ouch!

That may be the saddest thing I've ever read.

And unlike your dad, *you* lost money running casinos, which is nearly impossible to do unless you have a *very* exceptional brain. I mean, having a casino license is like owning a golden egg-laying goose. You're pretty much set for life unless you dry-hump it to death. Which you apparently did. Metaphorically, of course.

Love,
Pennyfarthing

May 8, 2019

- Trump claims executive privilege over the full unredacted Mueller report.
- The House Judiciary Committee votes to hold Attor-

- ney General William Barr in contempt of Congress for failing to hand over the unredacted Mueller report.
- *The Washington Post*'s Dana Milbank announces that the White House has revoked his press credentials. In a column for *The Post*, he writes, "I was part of a mass purge of 'hard pass' holders after the White House implemented a new standard that designated as unqualified almost the entire White House press corps, including all seven of The Post's White House correspondents. White House officials then chose which journalists would be granted 'exceptions.'"

May 9, 2019

- Charles Leerhsen, who ghostwrote *Trump: Surviving at the Top* for the future pr*sident, writes a column saying Trump was a terrible businessman who mostly just looked at fabric swatches: "But the main thing about fabric swatches was that they were within his comfort zone — whereas, for example, the management of hotels and airlines clearly wasn't."

From the Desk of Aldous J. Pennyfarthing
To: Donald Trump, slack man fever

Dear Pr*sident Assclown,

Ha ha ha ha ha ha ha ha ha ha ha!

Fabric swatches.

Wipes away tear

Ha ha ha ha ha ha ha ha ha ha ha!

I *do* find it a little surprising that picking out fabric swatches is within your comfort zone, though. I'd say you overestimated your aptitude for that as tragically as you did your qualifications for the presidency, which are pretty much limited to being over 35 years old, carbon-based, and only *mostly* dead.

I mean, I've seen pictures of your apartment. It looks like the goose who laid the golden egg had explosive diarrhea. That gauche salmagundi of gold leaf and godawful taste would have given *Liberace* seizures.

The fucking thing looks like Nero's outhouse, for shit's sake. Sheesh.

Love,
Pennyfarthing

◆ ◆ ◆

May 10, 2019

- After trade talks between the U.S. and China break down, Trump raises tariffs on $200 billion of Chinese goods. He later tweets, "Tariffs will make our Country MUCH STRONGER, not weaker. Just sit back and watch! In the meantime, China should not renegotiate deals with the U.S. at the last minute. This is not the Obama Administration, or the Administration of Sleepy Joe, who let China get away with 'murder!'"
- Trump also tweets, "Talks with China continue in a very congenial manner - there is absolutely no need to rush - as Tariffs are NOW being paid to the United States by China of 25% on 250 Billion Dollars worth of goods & products. These massive payments go directly to the Treasury of the U.S."

From the Desk of Aldous J. Pennyfarthing
To: Donald Trump, angry wankpuffin

Dear Pr*sident Assclown,

So despite having personally precipitated the perpetual pud-punching contest that is our current trade war with China, you *still* don't know how tariffs work.

For the 250 billionth time, CHINA IS NOT PAYING THEM! WE ARE!

It's a tax on *consumers*, King Cockwomble!

Er, never mind. You won't understand that word. It's a wholly foreign term to you.

I'll try again.

It's a tax on *gullible marks*, King Cockwomble!

Read a fucking book, you oafish, fleshy wad of id. We'd all benefit.

Love,
Pennyfarthing

May 13, 2019

- Trump's trade war with China continues as the country announces it will impose tariffs on $60 billion of U.S. goods.

May 14, 2019

- During a rally in Louisiana, Trump claims he's seen piles of bald eagles underneath windmills: "You want to see a bird cemetery? Go under a windmill sometime. You will see the saddest, you got every type of bird. You know, in California you go to jail for five years if you kill a bald eagle. You go under a windmill, you see them all over the place. Not a good situation."

From the Desk of Aldous J. Pennyfarthing
To: Donald Trump, the spittle rascal

Dear Pr*sident Assclown,

I *don't* want to see a bird cemetery, but thanks for asking.

Of course, this raises a key question. And that question is this:

What kind of fucking cemeteries are you visiting that you see piles of bodies lying around everywhere? I'm not sure what you've been doing with your Sunday afternoons, but dude … that's no cemetery.

So …

> 1) I don't believe you've ever visited a cemetery, because dead people can't do a thing for you. Unless your dad was accidentally buried with his safety deposit box key, you're not going anywhere near a grave. (Though if he had been buried with it I have no doubt you'd have jimmied open his regal sarcophagus with your mother's artificial hip and one or more of her femurs. And yes, I *do* know that she died after he did.)
> 2) Why would you ever visit a windmill when you're convinced that they cause cancer?
> 3) You see every type of bird, huh? I know you love to exaggerate, but there are approximately 18,000 species of birds in the world. I understand you and your EPA are trying to get that down to a far more manageable 20 or so (I mean, who really needs more than one species of fucking finch?), but the fact remains — what you said is nearly as impossible as your claim that you graduated at the head of your class at Wharton.
> 4) I really want you to back up this claim. Include all relevant citations and any photographs or other forms of

> electronic media you'd like to submit as evidence: "You go under a windmill, you see [bald eagles] all over the place." The only place you've ever seen a pile of dead birds is in a KFC bucket wedged between your heaving, oleaginous, 5,000-BTU moobs. This simply didn't — and doesn't — happen.

Oh, and I love this quote, too:

> "But that's what they were counting on, wind. And when the wind doesn't blow, you don't watch television that night. Your wife said, 'What the hell did you get me into with this Green New Deal, Charlie?'"

You should have been a stand-up comic. Not because you'd have been any good at it, but because you'd have died in obscurity in an alley with a heroin syringe sticking out of your arm and one of Gallagher's watermelon hammers mysteriously shoved up your ass. Now *that* would have been the best of all possible worlds — much better than this curdled ape placenta of a universe we're living in now.

By the way, if I ever do see a stack of bald eagles piled up like cordwood under a windmill, not only will I apologize profusely, I'll remove my small intestines with a Play-Doh scissors and use them to zip line into a Walmart Build-A-Bear Stuffing Station on Black Friday.

Love,
Pennyfarthing

May 17, 2019

- Treasury Secretary Steven Mnuchin says he won't

comply with a House subpoena to hand over six years of Donald Trump's tax returns.

May 19, 2019

- Trump tweets, "If Iran wants to fight, that will be the official end of Iran. Never threaten the United States again!"
- *The New York Times* reports that "[a]nti-money laundering specialists at Deutsche Bank recommended in 2016 and 2017 that multiple transactions involving legal entities controlled by Donald J. Trump and his son-in-law, Jared Kushner, be reported to a federal financial-crimes watchdog."
- After Rep. Justin Amash (R-Michigan) calls for Trump's impeachment, Trump tweets, "Never a fan of @justinamash, a total lightweight who opposes me and some of our great Republican ideas and policies just for the sake of getting his name out there through controversy. … Justin is a loser who sadly plays right into our opponents hands!"

May 20, 2019

- In response to a House subpoena for former White House counsel Don McGahn, Press Secretary Sarah Huckabee Sanders writes, "The Department of Justice has provided a legal opinion stating that, based on long-standing, bipartisan, and constitutional precedent, the former counsel to the president cannot

May 22, 2019

- Trump storms out of a planned infrastructure meeting with Nancy Pelosi and Chuck Schumer. In a Rose Garden press conference a few minutes later, Trump says, "Instead of walking in happily into a meeting, I walk in to people who just said I was doing a cover-up. I don't do cover-ups." A photo of Trump's crib notes for the press conference later reveals that he'd written, "Dems have no achomlishments."

From the Desk of Aldous J. Pennyfarthing
To: Donald Trump, unnaturally hued Muppet

Dear Pr*sident Assclown,

Let's see, several of the Democratic candidates for president are bilingual. In fact, one of them — Pete Buttigieg — speaks *seven* languages.

Imagine that.

And you?

You *kind* of speak English and are also nearly fluent in Cookie Monster.

"Mmmm. Dems have no a*chom*lishments! Me want coooookeee for Pesident Tump. BIG COOOOOOKEEEEE! Me best pesident in *whoooooole* country!"

And you don't do cover-ups? Dude, that's *all* you do. Yeah, I know you're really fucking bad at them, but that doesn't mean you don't try.

I mean, if you don't do cover-ups, what's with that yeti merkin on your head? Why do you look like a 600-pound Chicken McNugget covered in bee pollen?

And what was with the porn star and the *Playboy* model?

And the Mueller report? There was more obstruction in that thing than a Packer fan's colon.

Also, *The Washington Post* has chronicled more than 10,000 of your lies while you've been pr*sident. They had to create a new category — The Bottomless Pinocchio —*just for you*. Your supporters swallow more lies than trans fats.

If you worked *any other job* you would have been fired years ago, but because you only have the most important job in the world, it's fine, apparently.

So just who are you trying to fool, you pendulous llama tit? Because *most* of us are onto you.

Love,
Pennyfarthing

May 23, 2019

- Trump gives Attorney General William Barr authority to selectively declassify government secrets related to the investigation into Russian interference in the 2016 election.
- *The Washington Post* reports that Trump has repeatedly tried to steer a border wall contract to a company whose CEO is a Republican donor and a frequent Fox News guest. *The Post* notes that "[t]he push for a specific company has alarmed military commanders and DHS officials."

- Trump tweets, "Rex Tillerson, a man who is 'dumb as a rock' and totally ill prepared and ill equipped to be Secretary of State, made up a story (he got fired) that I was out-prepared by Vladimir Putin at a meeting in Hamburg, Germany. I don't think Putin would agree. Look how the U.S. is doing!"

May 24, 2019

- Trump declares a national security "emergency" in order to bypass Congress and ship arms to Saudi Arabia. In a letter to Sen. James Risch, chair of the Senate Foreign Relations Committee, Secretary of State Mike Pompeo writes, "I have determined that an emergency exists which requires the proposed sale in the national security interest of the United States, and, thus, waives the congressional review requirements."

May 25, 2019

- Trump tweets, "North Korea fired off some small weapons, which disturbed some of my people, and others, but not me. I have confidence that Chairman Kim will keep his promise to me, & also smiled when he called Swampman Joe Bidan [sic] a low IQ individual, & worse. Perhaps that's sending me a signal?"

From the Desk of Aldous J. Pennyfarthing
To: Donald Trump, Brave Sir Knob'n

Dear Pr*sident Assclown,

Ugh. This again.

You make it sound like Kim Jong Un is firing BBs at starlings. These are *ballistic missiles*, you bulbous fuck.

So who are you pointing your voluminous rage boner at today? Our sworn enemy North Korea, which has been saber-rattling with all the incandescent tiger-blood energy it can muster? Oh, no. "Swampman Joe Bidan," of course!

By the way, your monomaniacal obsession with Biden has been more all-consuming than your quixotic crusade to unmask the scoundrel who invented crudités, and yet you *still* can't spell his name.

What the fuck, man? If you keep this up the makers of Adderall are going to fucking *sue* you.

By the way, Swampman Joe Bidan is my least favorite DC character ever. Worse than Aquaman, for fuck's sake. Doesn't mean they won't make a movie about him, of course. Maybe Ben Affleck can take another shot at playing a superhero.

Love,
Pennyfarthing

◆ ◆ ◆

May 27, 2019

- While visiting Japan, noted aircraft carrier expert Donald Trump calls for a return to steam catapults on the Navy's carriers. He also wishes members of the Japanese military a "happy Memorial Day."

From the Desk of Aldous J. Pennyfarthing
To: Donald Trump, rancid spunknugget

Dear Pr*sident Assclown,

So did Kushner accompany you on your Japan trip? Because the last thing they want to see is another fat man and little boy.

So, okay, you wished members of the Japanese military a "happy Memorial Day." No biggie. I mean, it totally makes sense, right? Deep down, everyone wants to be an American. Well, everyone who doesn't want to be miniaturized with a CIA shrink-ray and gingerly nestled inside Vladimir Putin's oily Russian pubic mane like a newly hatched hummingbird.

But, whatever. I mean, you're the same guy who wants to force Walmart to say "Merry Christmas" to Muslims, Jews, and atheists. Why not a hale and hearty "happy Memorial Day!" to the country we bombed the shit out of that one time? … Er, two times.
Not that we didn't have our reasons but — *psssst* — it's *not their holiday*.

Other countries have their own cultures, traditions, and special commemorations. I realize you rarely go anywhere except McDonald's, but *even they're different in different countries*. There's a reason you can't get a McRib sandwich in Abu Dhabi, and it's not just because it tastes like a New Orleans longshoreman's asshole.

Oh, and why do you think you know more about aircraft carrier catapults than people who have dedicated their lives to trivial matters like, I don't know, aircraft carrier catapult design? Please stop trying to be an expert in things. Unless I need to know how to shoehorn Mike Pence inside my sigmoid colon using minimal lubrication — and I really doubt that will come up anytime soon, if ever — I don't see how you can really help me with anything.

Love,
Pennyfarthing

May 29, 2019

- Quartz.com reports that Trump's golf cart rental expenses have come to $500,000 since he was sworn in — more than the annual presidential salary he says he's not taking.
- Several news outlets report that Navy officials attempted to hide the U.S.S. John McCain from Trump during the pr*sident's visit to Japan. In addition, members of the ship's crew were not invited to Trump's speech. Trump denies he asked anyone to keep the ship out of sight but later says whoever did was "well-meaning."
- In a statement summarizing his report on Russian interference in the 2016 election, special counsel Robert Mueller says, "[A]s set forth in the report, after that investigation if we had had confidence that the president clearly did not commit a crime we would have said so."

May 30, 2019

- A court filing reveals that GOP strategist Thomas Hofeller, who had been part of the Trump administration's push for adding a citizenship question to the 2020 census, wrote a 2015 report concluding that the question would be "advantageous to Republicans and Non-Hispanic Whites." Hofeller died in 2018, and his daughter later found the incriminating information on his computer.
- Several media outlets report that North Korea executed five officials who were involved in February's failed U.S.-North Korea summit in Hanoi. On May 5, when asked about rumors that Kim Jong Un had exe-

cuted his negotiators, a smiling Secretary of State Mike Pompeo said, "Just as President Trump gets to decide who his negotiators will be, Chairman Kim will get to make his own decisions about who he asks to have these conversations."
- Trump finally admits Russia had a key role in the 2016 elections, tweeting, "Russia, Russia, Russia! That's all you heard at the beginning of this Witch Hunt Hoax. And now Russia has disappeared because I had nothing to do with Russia helping me to get elected."
- Trump threatens to impose a 5 percent tariff "on all goods imported from Mexico" if the country doesn't fix our immigration problem.
- When asked if he's worried about impeachment, Trump says, "I can't imagine the courts allowing it. I've never gone into it — I never thought that would even be possible to be using that word. To me it's a dirty word, the word 'impeach.' It's a dirty, filthy, disgusting word. ... You know, it's high crimes *and*, not with or 'or' — it's high crimes and misdemeanors. There was no high crime and there was no misdemeanor. So how do you impeach based on that?"

From the Desk of Aldous J. Pennyfarthing
To: Donald Trump, Putin's precious

Dear Pr*sident Assclown,

Wait, let me see if I can get this straight. Because I'm not a stable genius, like you.

You think that you can commit high crimes, but as long as you don't *also* commit misdemeanors, you're just fine? How else to interpret this tasty soupçon of cray-cray?

> "You know, it's high crimes *and*, not with or 'or' — it's high crimes and misdemeanors."

Okay, fine. So the high crime is that you're a traitorous pro-Putin puppet who engaged in systematic obstruction of the investigation into your seditious behavior, and the misdemeanor is your whale-scrotum-like chin flap. Is *that* enough?

You can't possibly be this stupid, can you? That's not a rhetorical question. I really want an answer. Because I prayed we'd never see another high-profile politician as dumb as Sarah Palin, and God answered my prayer with you. That's like asking God to cure my head cold and then watching my dick fall down my pant leg and through a sewer grate just as I'm saying, "Amen."

Thanks, God! You work in *extremely* mysterious ways.

And on the very same day that that incandescent fusillade of horse apples disgorged from your head, you tweeted *this*:

> "Russia, Russia, Russia! That's all you heard at the beginning of this Witch Hunt Hoax…And now Russia has disappeared because I had nothing to do with Russia helping me to get elected."

Thanks for finally admitting Russia helped get you elected. But I doubt you really intended to do that. Maybe you need someone smarter than you to proofread your tweets. Shouldn't be hard to find such a person. Just check Craigslist. Literally anyone selling used patio furniture would qualify.

Love,
Pennyfarthing

June 2, 2019

- In a tweet, Trump claims he never called Duchess of Sussex Meghan Markle "nasty," even though he was caught on tape saying exactly that.

June 3, 2019

- Just prior to landing in the U.K., Trump tweets, ".@SadiqKhan, who by all accounts has done a terrible job as Mayor of London, has been foolishly 'nasty' to the visiting President of the United States, by far the most important ally of the United Kingdom. He is a stone cold loser who should focus on crime in London, not me."
- A pathetically small crowd gathers to greet Trump's motorcade during his visit to London.
- Trump visits Westminster Abbey's Poets' Corner — a renowned cultural landmark where literary giants such as William Shakespeare, Charles Dickens, the Bronte sisters, Geoffrey Chaucer, Jane Austen, and Lord Byron are either buried or memorialized — and asks what the flooring is made of.
- Trump wears an ill-fitting tux to a state banquet with the royal family at Buckingham Palace.

From the Desk of Aldous J. Pennyfarthing
To: Donald Trump, Biffy the Empire Slayer

Dear Pr*sident Assclown,

Hooooooooleeeeeeee shit-crumpets.

What the fuck is wrong with you, you excrescent jigger of monkey clap? We spent the past 243 years showing Mother England that we can govern ourselves just fine, thank you, and you go and fuck it up in one day.

What the fuck were you wearing at that state dinner? You looked like 400 pounds of pig anus shoved into a 200-pound sausage casing. Jesus Christ, Mr. Creosote. I guess your tailors were well out of walkie-talkie range of each other when they were draping that Hieronymus Bosch monstrosity onto the far-flung reaches of your beached-manatee carcass. The Queen looks *frightened* in that photo of y'all together. She probably thought this was the last stop on a monarch-eating tour of Europe.

And why are you provoking the mayor of London, of all people? Is it because he's a Muslim? So what? You're the phoniest Christian on the planet, and the Queen welcomed you with open arms — which were not nearly long enough to wrap around that Macy's Opus balloon of a torso, apparently.

But this was by far my favorite part of your adventure, from a dispatch by reporter Rob Crilly:

> POTUS re-emerged into the lantern of Westminster Abbey at 15.42 to see Poets' Corner.
>
> He paused at the white marble slab commemorating Lord Byron, the poet politician, and asked what stone the flooring was made from.

Fuck. Me.

Who gets to tell John Smith that the colony he founded has gone tits up?

I ... can't ... even.

Love,
Pennyfarthing

June 4, 2019

- NBC News reports that the Trump administration approved the transfer of nuclear technology to Saudi Arabia just 16 days after the murder of U.S.-based jour-

- nalist Jamal Khashoggi.
- Huge crowds gather in London to protest Trump's visit to the U.K.
- The White House instructs former Trump aide Hope Hicks not to comply with a congressional subpoena seeking documents related to her tenure.
- According to Michael Wolff's new book, *Siege: Trump Under Fire*, former White House adviser Steve Bannon thinks Trump will start to lose followers when they discover he's "not the billionaire he said he was, [but] just another scumbag."

June 5, 2019

- Trump tweets, "I kept hearing that there would be 'massive' rallies against me in the UK, but it was quite the opposite. The big crowds, which the Corrupt Media hates to show, were those that gathered in support of the USA and me. They were big & enthusiastic as opposed to the organized flops!"
- In a crazy interview with British "journalist" Piers Morgan, Trump defends his decision not to serve in Vietnam by saying it was "very far away" and "nobody ever heard of the country."

June 6, 2019

- During an interview in front of a cemetery full of fallen American heroes, Trump says, "Nancy Pelosi, I call her Nervous Nancy, Nancy Pelosi doesn't talk about it. Nancy Pelosi is a disaster, okay? She's a disaster. Let her do what she wants, you know what? I think they're in big trouble." He made the comments just minutes before heading to an event commemorating the 75th anniversary of D-Day.

◆ ◆ ◆

June 7, 2019

- Trump tweets, "For all of the money we are spending, NASA should NOT be talking about going to the Moon - We did that 50 years ago. They should be focused on the much bigger things we are doing, including Mars (of which the Moon is a part), Defense and Science!"

From the Desk of Aldous J. Pennyfarthing
To: Donald Trump, disgrace cadet

Dear Pr*sident Assclown,

That's, uh, quite a tweet. Please tell me you didn't just find out about the moon landing. Please.

Okay, so here's what you said on December 11, 2017, shortly before your brain was colonized by miniature space crustaceans:

> "The directive I'm signing today will refocus America's space program on human exploration and discovery. It marks an important step in returning American astronauts to the moon for the first time since 1972, for long-term exploration and use. This time we will not only plant our flag and leave our footprint — we will establish a foundation for an eventual mission to Mars and perhaps someday to many worlds beyond."

Frankly, that doesn't sound like you at all, but it's right there on NBC News' webpage.

Of course, *this* sounds exactly like you:

> "For all of the money we are spending, NASA should NOT be talking about going to the Moon - We did that 50 years ago. They should be focused on the much bigger things we are doing, including Mars (of which the Moon is a part), Defense and Science!"

One of those paragraphs is a carefully crafted policy statement, and the other is pretty much what I hear in my head when I read the backs of cereal boxes while drunk. Gee, I wonder which one represents your true thoughts on space exploration.

Now, a lot of people have made fun of you for tweeting "including Mars (of which the moon is a part)." *A lot*. Like, you wouldn't fucking believe how many. I mean, it's pretty much the only thing people are talking about today. I think the pope interrupted morning Mass to retweet it with a crying-barf-face emoji.

But I sort of get what you're saying. You have to establish a moon base so you can make a low-gravity launch from the moon to Mars. I think that's the plan, anyway. I didn't look it up or anything. I figured it out all by myself with my non-Adderall-soaked brain.

But this part confuses me. In the same tweet where you talk about the moon mission being part of the Mars mission, you emphatically state that we should NOT be talking about going to the moon. You capitalized it and everything.

So the moon (mission, that is) is part of the Mars (mission). And yet you think we *shouldn't* go to the moon? So are you *actually* saying the moon is part of Mars? (Which, for the record, it isn't.)

That can't be right, can it?

And why am I trying to make sense out of something that spilled like a tauntaun's steamy entrails from the expired, moldering tin of anchovy paste that is your mind?

I think I'll just quit while I'm ahead. Or behind. Not sure which, honestly.

Love,
Pennyfarthing

❖ ❖ ❖

June 8, 2019

- Trump tweets, "Little @DonnyDeutsch, whose show, like his previous shoebiz [sic] tries, is a disaster, has been saying that I had been a friend of his. This is false. He, & separately @ErinBurnett, used to BEG me to be on episodes of the Apprentice (both were bad), but that was it. Hardly knew him, other than to know he was, and is, a total Loser. When he makes statements about me, they are made up, he knows nothing!"

❖ ❖ ❖

June 10, 2019

- Former Nixon White House counsel John Dean testifies in front of the House Judiciary Committee, prompting Republicans everywhere to lose their shit.
- In an interview with CNBC, Trump claims that China has "lost $15 to $20 trillion in value since the day I was elected." In response, FactCheck.org notes that "Credit Suisse's annual analysis of total household wealth shows that China's went up nearly $5.3 trillion between the end of 2016 and the middle of 2018, the latest data available."
- Several news outlets report that a "friendship tree" Trump and French President Emmanuel Macron had planted on the White House lawn in April 2018 died

while in quarantine.

From the Desk of Aldous J. Pennyfarthing
To: Donald Trump, the French disease

Dear Pr*sident Assclown,

So does everything you touch with your creepy corn husk doll hands have to die? Friendship trees, our country's honor and dignity, the economy. And God knows how many years you've shaved off your wee willie winky with your unwelcome attentions.

No wonder Melania doesn't want to touch you, like, ever. She'd prefer not to melt into a sad puddle of dive-bar egg brine and couture.

I honestly can't think of a more apt metaphor for your impact on the world and our vital alliances than a "friendship tree" you ceremonially planted — and then had uprooted and placed in a closet — dying.

Actually, that seems an apt metaphor for your entire life. I don't know you personally, but it's been my sense that you have no actual "friends" — just victims, co-conspirators, and pathetic, unwitting future victims (i.e., idiot hangers-on).

I mean, you're more universally loathed than the massing heap of discarded organs and tissue that used to be Dick Cheney.

Seriously, other than Ivanka and Jared, show me one person who knows you personally and doesn't hate your guts. You've tormented your other kids relentlessly and have viciously insulted or thrown everyone else who ever trusted you under the bus.

Prove me wrong, man. Show me one genuine friend. And those "hundreds of friends" you claim you lost during 9/11 don't count. As you well know, they were imaginary.

Love,
Pennyfarthing

◆ ◆ ◆

June 11, 2019

- While speaking with reporters outside the White House, Trump says he's secured a secret immigration deal with Mexico. He waves around a piece of paper that supposedly has the details of the agreement printed on it, but he refuses to show it to anyone. Mexico later releases a copy of the document, which is simply an agreement to begin discussing an agreement.

◆ ◆ ◆

June 12, 2019

- When asked if national security officials will be in the room during Trump's upcoming meeting with Vladimir Putin, ape goes Trump-shit: "Well it's probably easier because you people are so untrusting, so it's probably better. Would you like to be in the room? Okay? Would you like to be? I can imagine you would be. I think it's probably easier if we have people in the room because you people don't trust anything."
- When ABC's George Stephanopoulos asks Trump whether his campaign would accept damaging information about his opponent from a foreign government, Trump replies, "I think you might want to listen. There isn't anything wrong with listening. If somebody called from a country, Norway, [and said], 'We have information on your opponent' — oh, I think I'd want to hear it.' He also says he wouldn't neces-

sarily alert the FBI: "It's not an interference. They have information, I think I'd take it. If I thought there was something wrong, I'd go maybe to the FBI, if I thought there was something wrong. But when somebody comes up with oppo research, right, they come up with oppo research, 'oh let's call the FBI.' The FBI doesn't have enough agents to take care of it. When you go and talk, honestly, to congressmen, they all do it, they always have, and that's the way it is. It's called oppo research."

- After Russia contradicts Trump's assertion that the country had "removed most of their people from Venezuela," Trump says, "Well, let's just see who's right. You know what you're gonna do? You're gonna see in the end who's right. And we'll see who is right. … Ultimately I'm always right."
- In response to a Geraldo Rivera tweet about Russian collusion, Trump tweets, "is = if (Spell)! Not like Chris."

From the Desk of Aldous J. Pennyfarthing
To: Donald Trump, The Wanko Kid

Dear Pr*sident Assclown,

What's the frequency, Kenneth?

Is this thing on?

"is = if (Spell)! Not like Chris."

Okay, Zapf Dingbats — you're either a lot smarter than everyone else or *waaaaaaaaaayyyyyyyy* the fuck dumber.

Also, that's a fuckuvalota crazy for one day. You tweeted that cryptic weirdo nonsense on the same day you said you were ultimately "always" right, lamented that the press doesn't trust anything at face value (maybe because you always lie, and verifying stuff is kind of their job?), and — this one's a doozy — asserted that you'd happily welcome election interference from foreign governments.

Uh, have you been paying attention to *anything* the past two years? No? Okay, let's move on then.

What the fuck was that tweet? If I didn't know better, I'd think you're workshopping a new improv character called Strokey the Clown.

I'd like to think I'm pretty good at translating your turgid gibberish into the Queen's English, but this one has even me baffled. Did one of your fabled covfefe boys write it?

What's the Rosetta stone that's going to allow 24th century Trump scholars (bwaha ha ha ha ha ha, *Trump* scholars) to decipher this? They'll be parsing this like the Zapruder film before throwing up their hands in frustration, exhuming your body, and finding incontrovertible proof that there were actually more worms burrowing through your brain *before* you died than after.

Or something like that. Frankly, I doubt anyone will give two shits about you five minutes after Washington expectorates you back onto the sidewalk outside the Atlantic City Dunkin' Donuts. If it were up to me, I'd tape over every single inch of video from your White House tenure with reruns of *Small Wonder*.

But that's just me. I'm sure you'll be very beloved once you're gone. No one's gonna think you were nuts or anything. Just try not to think about it.

Love,
Pennyfarthing

❖ ❖ ❖

June 13, 2019

- Trump announces via Twitter that White House Press Secretary Sarah Huckabee Sanders will leave her post at the end of the month.
- The U.S. Office of Special Counsel says Kellyanne Conway should be fired over her repeated violations of the Hatch Act, which prohibits administration employees from participating in political activities while performing official duties: "As a highly visible member of the Administration, Ms. Conway's violations, if left unpunished, send a message to all federal employees that they need not abide by the Hatch Act's restrictions. Her actions thus erode the principal foundation of our democratic system—the rule of law." In an interview with *Fox & Friends*, Trump later says, "No, I'm not going to fire her. I think she's a terrific person."
- Trump tweets, "I meet and talk to 'foreign governments' every day. I just met with the Queen of England (U.K.), the Prince of Whales, the P.M. of the United Kingdom, the P.M. of Ireland, the President of France and the President of Poland. We talked about 'Everything!'"

From the Desk of Aldous J. Pennyfarthing
To: Donald Trump, The Royal Wee-brain

Dear Pr*sident Assclown,

Prince of Whales, huh? You'll have to help me out, because it's been a while since I've seen *Finding Nemo*. Which one was he?

But, okay. Maybe that's not fair. Not everyone is a great speller. My dad, for instance. He couldn't spell very well. But he was endlessly curious, had a mind for science, and was a brilliant engineer.

You, on the other hand, are endlessly spurious and have a mind for Funyuns.

And here's another difference. My father was a voracious reader, whereas you pretend to have written best-selling books that you in fact did not write. And you can't be bothered to read a briefing that's longer than half a page.

So while you don't even have the sense to let an intern proof your insane ramblings and have apparently confused Prince Charles with Aquaman, that's far from the only way you're stupid. You are a steaming paella of derp, and our country may never recover from it.

Can we sell ourselves back to the U.K.? While our country is no doubt worth hundreds of trillions of dollars, at this point I'd let it go for an Arthur Treacher's Fish & Chips franchise and a solemn promise that you'll spend the next 10 years in the Tower of London eating porridge and tripe. And not the good tripe. A generic knock-off brand. From China.

Love,
Pennyfarthing

June 14, 2019

- Trump signs an executive order directing all federal agencies to cut their advisory boards by at least a third.

June 15, 2019

- Trump tweets, "The Trump Economy is setting records, and has a long way up to go. However, if anyone but me takes over in 2020 (I know the competi-

tion very well), there will be a Market Crash the likes of which has not been seen before! KEEP AMERICA GREAT."
- *The New York Times* reports that intelligence officials withheld information about a cyberattack against Russia's electrical grid from Trump because they were worried he would leak it to foreign officials.

From the Desk of Aldous J. Pennyfarthing
To: Donald Trump, powdered bologna shart

Dear Pr*sident Assclown,

In my experience it's always a good sign when underlings withhold key information from the boss because they're terrified of what he might do. It means you've earned their respect. So, yeah, keep it up, Taint Petersburg.

Of course, it's probably a good thing our government limits your exposure to Vladimir Putin or you'd end up dry-humping his leg until it looked like a Coney Island mini golf pencil.

But thank God we didn't elect Hillary Clinton. Whew. We really dodged a bullet on that one. Who knows what *she* would have done with classified information? Probably would have spilled everything to Angela Merkel and Theresa May at a pajama party during a game of truth or dare or something.

Love,
Pennyfarthing

June 16, 2019
- Trump fires some of his pollsters following the leak of internal polling that shows him trailing Democrat Joe Biden in several key swing states.
- Trump tweets, "A poll should be done on which is the

more dishonest and deceitful newspaper, the Failing New York Times or the Amazon (lobbyist) Washington Post! They are both a disgrace to our Country, the Enemy of the People, but I just can't seem to figure out which is worse? The good news is that at the end of 6 years, after America has been made GREAT again and I leave the beautiful White House (do you think the people would demand that I stay longer? KEEP AMERICA GREAT), both of these horrible papers will quickly go out of business & be forever gone!"
- ABC News reveals footage of Trump freaking out at his chief of staff, Mick Mulvaney, for coughing during an interview.
- In an interview with ABC's George Stephanopoulos, Trump says, "Look, Article II, I would be allowed to fire Robert Mueller. Assuming I did all the things ... number one, I didn't. He wasn't fired. ... But more importantly, Article II allows me to do whatever I want. Article II would have allowed me to fire him."

June 17, 2019

- Trump tweets, ".@FoxNews Polls are always bad for me. They were against Crooked Hillary also. Something weird going on at Fox. Our polls show us leading in all 17 Swing States. For the record, I didn't spend 30 hours with @abcnews, but rather a tiny fraction of that. More Fake News @BretBaier"

June 18, 2019

- At his official 2020 campaign kickoff in Orlando, Florida, Trump says that, if he's reelected, his administration will cure cancer and AIDS. "We will come up with the cures to many, many problems, to many, many diseases, including cancer and others. And we're getting closer all the time."

From the Desk of Aldous J. Pennyfarthing
To: Donald Trump, the primary reason for my do-not-resuscitate order

Dear Pr*sident Assclown,

Okay, I'd love to see a cure for cancer and AIDS in my lifetime, but I'd also like to not have my viscera lassoed around my neck by Master Blaster in Thunderdome.

Such a tough choice.

How close are you to curing cancer, anyway? Or are you saying you're going to *start* trying to cure cancer only if you're re-elected? Because that would be, er, kind of irresponsible.

So if, say, Joe Biden, whose son actually *died* of cancer, is elected, he'll just ignore cancer and all research will stop? Sounds legit.

Or are you saying you have some sort of cancer-'n'-AIDS curin' secret that you'll wrest from your windy asshole in November 2020? Call me crazy, but I don't quite believe you.

By the way, your son (the dumb one ... er, no, the *other* dumb one) — at *the very same rally* in which you vowed to cure cancer — said this:

> "What was the good one last week? Remember? Joe Biden comes out, 'Well, if you elect me president, I'm going to cure cancer.' Wow, why the hell didn't you do that over the last 50 years, Joe?"

Ha ha ha ha ha ha!

And here you were:

> "We will come up with the cures to many, many problems, to many, many diseases, including cancer and others. And we're getting closer all the time."

And here was Biden:

> "A lot of you understand what loss is and when loss occurs, you know that people come up to you and tell you 'I understand' if you lose a husband, a wife, a son, a daughter, a family member. That's why I've worked so hard in my career to make sure that — I promise you if I'm elected president, you're going to see the single most important thing that changes America, we're going to cure cancer."

To be fair, those are similar promises. But whereas Biden was likely overcome with grief, you're most likely overcome with an increasingly voluminous series of plastic bags filled with hairspray fumes.

So not *quite* the same thing. Also, you're a gormless fucking twatflap. So there's that.

Love,
Pennyfarthing

June 19, 2019

- Trump presents the Presidential Medal of Freedom to "economist" Arthur Laffer, the godfather of trickle-down economics, co-author of *Trumponomics*, and the inventor of the infamous Laffer curve.
- EPA administrator Andrew Wheeler, a former coal lobbyist, rolls back Obama-era regulations on coal-fired power plants.

June 20, 2019

- After a *Time* photographer snaps a picture of a letter to Trump from Kim Jong Un, Trump appears to threaten the photographer with prison time: "Well, you can go to prison, instead, because if you use, if you use the photograph you took of the letter that I gave you …" After the reporter responds with, "I'm sorry, Mr. President. Were you threatening me with prison time?" Trump replies, "So go have fun with your story, because I'm sure it will be the 28th horrible story I have in *Time* magazine because I never, I mean, ha. It's incredible. With all I've done and the success I've had, the way that *Time* magazine writes is absolutely incredible."

June 21, 2019

- Writer E. Jean Carroll says Trump raped her in a department store dressing room in the mid-'90s. Trump later claims, "I've never met this person in my life"—though they were photographed together at least once.
- After Iran shoots down a U.S. drone, Trump orders an attack on the country but then backs down at the last minute. In a tweet, he explains, "On Monday they shot down an unmanned drone flying in International Waters. We were cocked & loaded to retaliate last night on 3 different sights when I asked, how many will die. 150 people, sir, was the answer from a General. 10 minutes before the strike I stopped it."

From the Desk of Aldous J. Pennyfarthing
To: Donald Trump, lazy bonespurs

Dear Pr*sident Assclown,

"You stopped the ill-advised war you almost singlehandedly started with your loutish, clodhopping fucknuttery" doesn't really fit on a cake, so I'll just say, "Congratulations. You fucked up a little less than I thought you would, Private Jizztart."

But don't think you should get any credit for this. It's like shitting in your own pants instead of the hot bar at Kroger. A victory ... relatively speaking.

Is now the right time to mention that Barack Obama had a handle on our Iran problem, and you stupidly abrogated our agreement with the country? Because don't think we've forgotten about that. Everyone without a blood vendetta against our 44th president and/or a pony keg's worth of adipose cascading down their rheumy, Adderall-wonky eyeballs could clearly see the nuclear agreement was working. And you've left us with a choice between war and, uh, letting Iran get a nuclear weapon.

By the way, crossing John Bolton is always a great idea. I don't think there's any chance that could come back to haunt you. Nosirree, blob.

And to be fair, I don't think this has anything to do with the rape accusation launched against you today, though some might see a wag-the-dog dynamic in all this. My theory? If you started a war every time you faced a credible rape accusation the planet would look like Deadpool's balls.

So, no. This is just the usual garden-variety stupidity. You don't need a reason for that.

Love,
Pennyfarthing

June 23, 2019

- In an interview with *Meet the Press*' Chuck Todd, Trump appears to claim yet again that millions of illegal votes cost him the popular vote: "I'm going to say something again that I think is controversial. There were a lot of votes cast that I don't believe."
- On *Meet the Press*, Trump brushes aside the vicious murder of journalist Jamal Khashoggi, saying, "Saudi Arabia is a big buyer of [U.S.] product. That means something to me. It's a big producer of jobs." He also says he might want to locate his presidential library on one of his own properties.
- Leaked Trump transition documents show that the team vetting top administration officials had cited numerous red flags.

June 24, 2019

- On Twitter, Trump appears to say he might stop protecting the Strait of Hormuz: "China gets 91% of its Oil from the Straight [sic], Japan 62%, & many other countries likewise. So why are we protecting the shipping lanes for other countries (many years) for zero compensation. All of these countries should be protecting their own ships on what has always been a dangerous journey."
- Trump signs an executive order imposing new sanctions on Iran.
- In response to writer E. Jean Carroll's allegation that Trump raped her in a New York department store in

the '90s, he says, "Number one, she's not my type. Number two, it never happened. It never happened, okay?"

June 25, 2019

- Asked if he has an exit strategy should a war break out with Iran, Trump says, "You're not going to need an exit strategy. I don't need exit strategies."
- *Highlights for Children* issues a statement lambasting Trump's family-separation policy.

From the Desk of Aldous J. Pennyfarthing
To: Donald Trump, the mad hater

Dear Pr*sident Assclown,

I never thought I'd see the day when *Highlights for Children* became the enemy of the people.

Or when the best way to reach the president of the United States would be through a children's magazine.

Here's just a portion of *Highlights*' scathing rebuke of, er, you:

> As a company that helps children become their best selves — curious, creative, caring, and confident — we want kids to understand the importance of having moral courage. Moral courage means standing up for what we believe is right, honest, and ethical — even when it is hard.
>
> Our company's core belief, stated each month in Highlights magazine, is that "Children are the world's most important people." This is a belief about ALL children.
>
> With this core belief in our minds and hearts, we

> denounce the practice of separating immigrant children from their families and urge our government to cease this activity, which is unconscionable and causes irreparable damage to young lives.

Well done, Goofus. This is quite an honor. Reminds me of the time Captain Kangaroo called Lyndon Johnson an execrable thundercunt.

That sound you hear is millions of clammy MAGA oafs, their slobbery St. Bernard mouths perdurably agape, straining to comprehend the latest editorial from *Highlights for Children*.

Let me know when you finally get to "unconscionable." I can help you sound it out.

Love,
Pennyfarthing

June 26, 2019

- Ahead of a meeting with Vladimir Putin at the upcoming G20 summit, Trump tells reporters, "I will have a very good conversation with him. What I say to him is none of your business."
- In a speech to the Faith & Freedom Coalition, Trump appears to suggest he's glad John McCain is dead and thinks he may be in hell: "We had the House of Representatives and the Senate, but we didn't have enough votes because it was very close. We needed 60 votes, and we had 51 votes. But sometimes, you know, we had a little hard time with a couple of them, right? Fortunately, they're gone now. They've gone on to greener pastures. Or, perhaps, far less green pastures, but they're gone. They're gone, Bill! Very happy they're gone. And we have great senators."

June 27, 2019

- Several media outlets report that former Secretary of State Rex Tillerson told the House Foreign Affairs Committee that Jared Kushner had set up a shadow operation and often left Tillerson out of the loop on geopolitical affairs. Tillerson also testified that Pr*sident Trump doesn't read briefing papers and is easily distracted.
- Calling the justification for adding a citizenship question to the 2020 census "contrived," the Supreme Court blocks the administration's attempt to add the question.

June 28, 2019

- At a human rights conference, former president Jimmy Carter says Trump is an illegitimate president who "was put into office because the Russians interfered."
- During a meeting between Trump and Vladimir Putin at the G20 Summit, a reporter asks Trump if he'll tell Putin not to meddle in the 2020 election. Trump sarcastically responds, "Yes, of course I will. Don't meddle in the election, President." He also jokes with Putin about eliminating journalists: "Get rid of them. Fake news is a great term, isn't it? You don't have this problem in Russia, but we do."
- At the G20 Summit, Trump says, "All of the leaders have come up and said it's incredible what's happened with the United States and they congratulate me and

congratulate the people of the United States."

From the Desk of Aldous J. Pennyfarthing
To: Donald Trump, international embarrassment

Dear Pr*sident Assclown,

Are you fucking kidding me with this?

> "All of the leaders have come up and said it's incredible what's happened with the United States and they congratulate me and congratulate the people of the United States."

Uh, okay. Sure.

If you can produce *even one* world leader who said this, I'll saw off the top of my next-door neighbor's head with a yard of garden twine, fill it with Jägermeister and horse semen, and quaff that shit like motherfucking Gimli bar-hopping in the Shire while a shithoused barn owl blows me in the loge section of the New York Metropolitan Opera.

That. Simply. Did. Not. Happen.

I mean, you lie so frequently and so facilely, it's crazy how fucking bad you are at it. They say that you need 10,000 hours of practice to be really great at anything. So let's see. Assuming you learned to speak when you were 7, I calculate that you've been lying pretty much nonstop for 578,160 hours. And yet you still suck at it.

You're ambitious, I grant you that. But this isn't an "I'm a racecar driver"-level lie. It's more like, "I invented the wheel." Or "I just nailed Danica Patrick." Or "I taught a legume how to knit Bavarian tea cozies."

Seriously, though. Our standing on the world stage has never been worse. It's like we went from being homecoming king to the kid who sneaks into the cafeteria every day before lunch to pee in the Tater Tots.

The only "incredible" thing about you or your administration is your amazing pair of gravity-complying moobs. They're otherworldly, honestly.

I suspect witchcraft.

Love,
Pennyfarthing

❖ ❖ ❖

June 29, 2019

- When asked about Vladimir Putin's remark that Western-style liberalism is "obsolete," Trump appears to suggest that "Western-style liberalism" refers to California politics: "He sees what's going on, I guess, if you look at what's happening in Los Angeles, where it's so sad to look, and what's happening in San Francisco and a couple of other cities, which are run by an extraordinary group of liberal people."

From the Desk of Aldous J. Pennyfarthing
To: Donald Trump, shrieky fucktrumpet

Dear Pr*sident Assclown,

I don't know what's more unnerving — the fact that you don't know what Western-style liberalism is or that it doesn't surprise me in the least that you don't know what Western-style liberalism is.

Vladimir Putin would fuck Lenin's corpse in the middle of Red Square with a Tickle Me Elmo up his ass if he could have even one city in his shithole empire that was as vibrant or wealthy as Los Angeles or San Francisco.

Moscow has three times Los Angeles' population and just two-thirds its GDP. Are you the president of the United States or vice chancellor of Russia? Maybe you should do some soul-searching and get back to us. (No, seriously, search for your soul. You going on a wild goose chase is exactly what this country needs right now.)

Love,
Pennyfarthing

◆ ◆ ◆

June 30, 2019

- Trump meets Kim Jong Un at the DMZ, becoming the first U.S. president to step foot in North Korea.
- Trump falsely claims that President Obama had begged to meet with Kim Jong Un but was rebuffed: "They couldn't have meetings. Nobody was going to meet. President Obama wanted to meet, and Chairman Kim would not meet him. The Obama administration was begging for a meeting. They were begging for meetings constantly. And Chairman Kim would not meet with him. And for some reason, we have a certain chemistry or whatever."

From the Desk of Aldous J. Pennyfarthing
To: Donald Trump, golden toilet god

Dear Pr*sident Assclown,

Okay, listen up, Jugs. None of that is true. President Obama did not beg Kim Jong Un for a meeting.

How do I know?

1) You say it happened.
2) No one else says it happened.
3) It's simply not the kind of thing Obama would ever do.
4) Begging Kim Jong Un for a meeting would be stupid,

and Obama is smart.

5) Did I mention that you say it happened? Yeah, I could have stopped there, honestly.

I'm not sure why you're bragging so much about meeting with Kim Jong Un. North Korea has been jonesing for a high-level meeting like this for years. Literally any president could have done this. They didn't because they weren't gullible dipshits who were dumber than their own haircuts.

Of course, to come to the conclusion that your North Korea policy is anything but a flaming mons pubis you'd have to stick your head so far up your own arse you'd see which kind of Girl Scout cookies you ate last night after getting high. And yet somehow you managed it.

That "certain chemistry" you feel between you and Kim Jong Un is him throwing acid in your face like a bucket of chum. In other words, you've given Kim a basketful of goodies he's always wanted and he's given up literally nothing.

"Art of the Deal" indeed.

For the record, here's what *The Washington Post*'s Fact Checker said about your claim:

> No public records or news articles show that Obama ever tried to meet with Kim. Former U.S. intelligence officials and experts on North Korea said they knew of no evidence for Trump's claim. Many of Obama's top advisers on North Korea said Trump's claim was false.
>
> In fact, Obama's strategy after 2012 was to escalate sanctions and avoid entreaties to North Korea. He very clearly told the world he was not interested in a meeting, but Trump did not get the message and earns Four Pinocchios.

That is, you simply made this up.

But we already knew that, didn't we?

Love,
Pennyfarthing

◆ ◆ ◆

July 1, 2019

- During an interview with Fox News' Tucker Carlson, Trump appears to say homelessness started two years ago: "It's a phenomenon that started two years ago. It's disgraceful. I'm going to maybe — I am looking at it very seriously."
- Trump says "brand-new Sherman tanks" will be part of the July 4 celebration at the National Mall. The U.S. military replaced the Sherman tank in the '50s.

From the Desk of Aldous J. Pennyfarthing
To: Donald Trump, daft dodger

Dear Pr*sident Assclown,

"Let's do the time warp again!"

So homelessness started two years ago and they're still making Sherman tanks. Way to be on top of things, Drip Van Tinkle.

Maybe next year your big Fourth of July celebration should just be you handing out Werther's Originals to bemused, creeped-out children.

So where to start? The fact that you apparently think homelessness is a new phenomenon or that you're going to have "new" Sherman tanks at your July 4 Paean to Thineself. That's enough crazy for a lifetime, and yet you accomplished it all in one day.

What other surprises do you have in store? Are you going to win the Nathan's Famous hot dog-eating contest on Coney Island? You know what? You should enter. And don't dip the buns in water like those other pussies. You have a maw like an industrial-grade wood chipper stuck inside a whale shark's throat. You could beat an Arby's roast beef slicer in a hot dog-eating contest, FFS.

Just keep shoving dogs down your esophagus until your windpipe shrinks to the size of a gravitational singularity. But remember. Only losers tap out. *Keep* going until you can see the light at the end of the tunnel — and your departed loved ones showing up to tell you what an irredeemable, fragrant trash barge you've been all your life.

Never give up — not until your purpling, tumescent shit-noggin has hoovered up a world-record 75 hot dogs in 10 minutes. Be all that you can be, man.

Now *that* would be an unforgettable July 4.

Love,
Pennyfarthing

◆ ◆ ◆

July 2, 2019

- *The Washington Post* reports that the National Park Service diverted $2.5 million earmarked for park improvements to Trump's July 4 celebration on the National Mall.

◆ ◆ ◆

July 3, 2019

- Trump tweets, "Iran has just issued a New Warning. Rouhani says that they will Enrich Uranium to 'any amount we want' if there is no new Nuclear Deal. Be careful with the threats, Iran. They can come back to bite you like nobody has been bitten before!"

July 4, 2019

- During his July 4 speech on the National Mall, Trump says, "The Continental Army suffered a bitter winter of Valley Forge, found glory across the waters of the Delaware, and seized victory from Cornwallis of Yorktown. Our army manned the air, it rammed the ramparts, it took over the airports, it did everything it had to do. And at Fort McHenry, under the rockets' red glare, it had nothing but victory. And when dawn came, their star-spangled banner waved defiant."

From the Desk of Aldous J. Pennyfarthing
To: Donald Trump, the weakest dink

Dear Pr*sident Assclown,

These are literally the lyrics Leslie Nielsen sang during the national anthem scene from *The Naked Gun*, aren't they? Never mind. I'll look it up later.

So, you used to make fun of Obama for reading off a teleprompter. But I don't think he needed it to remind him when the airplane was invented. But you used a teleprompter during *this* speech and somehow concocted Cornwallis in a Curtiss H-16.

Well done, Donorrhea.

Though your version of history is much more fun, I grant you that.

I kind of like the idea of Abraham Lincoln and Jefferson Davis going head to head in naked gay roller derby. Can you make that happen for us? Thanks in advance.

Oh, and after the army rammed the ramparts, did it ramp up its rampage or ram some ramen in a ramshackle rampole? These details are important.

Of course, Republicans gave you high marks for your July 4 speech because you didn't whip your dick out, put a tiny deerstalker cap on it, and declare it ambassador to the Klingon Empire. You just made up a story about airports during the Revolutionary War. And I can't begin to tell you how depressed I am knowing that's not even close to the stupidest thing you've ever said.

Love,
Pennyfarthing

❖ ❖ ❖

July 7, 2019

- On Twitter, Trump criticizes Brian Williams for making up stories: "Watching @FoxNews weekend anchors is worse than watching low ratings Fake News @CNN, or Lyin' Brian Williams (remember when he totally fabricated a War Story trying to make himself into a hero, & got fired. A very dishonest journalist!)"

❖ ❖ ❖

July 8, 2019

- Trump shares a fake Ronald Reagan quote from a spoof Twitter account. The quote, which accompanies a photo of Reagan shaking hands with a young Trump, says, "For the life of me, and I'll never know how to explain it, when I met that young man, I felt like I was the

- one shaking hands with a president."
- In a speech on environmental policy, Trump appears to take credit for raising awareness of forest management: "A lot of people are looking at forest management. It's a word that people didn't understand last year, and now they're getting it."
- After a series of leaked cables reveals that Kim Darroch, the U.K. ambassador to the U.S., believes that Trump is "inept," "clumsy," and "uniquely dysfunctional," Trump says, "We will no longer deal with him."

July 9, 2019

- Washington, D.C., mayor Muriel Bowser writes a letter to the White House saying Trump's July 4 celebration depleted the city's security fund: "Our projections indicate that the EPSF [Emergency Planning and Security Fund] will be depleted following your additional July 4th holiday activities and subsequent first amendment demonstrations. The accrued amount for the July 4th holiday totals approximately $1.7 million."
- *The New York Times* reports that 28 women were flown to a "calendar girl" competition at Mar-a-Lago in 1992. The party had been billed as a VIP event, but only Trump and Jeffrey Epstein attended.

From the Desk of Aldous J. Pennyfarthing
To: Donald Trump, Professor X-Rated

Dear Pr*sident Assclown,

My gawd, I feel like I need a chemical eyewash station in my living room just for reading the news. Do they have different calibrations? Because I want to set mine to "puree my forever-unclean eyeballs, if you please."

You are so fucking gross, dude.

So, yeah, this — from *The New York Times*:

> The year was 1992 and the event was a "calendar girl" competition, something that George Houraney, a Florida-based businessman who ran American Dream Enterprise, had organized at Mr. Trump's request.
>
> "I arranged to have some contestants fly in," Mr. Houraney recalled in an interview on Monday. "At the very first party, I said, 'Who's coming tonight? I have 28 girls coming.' It was him and Epstein."
>
> Mr. Houraney, who had just partnered with Mr. Trump to host events at his casinos, said he was surprised. "I said, 'Donald, this is supposed to be a party with V.I.P.s. You're telling me it's you and Epstein?'"

I think my hippocampus just curdled. Sorry, my brain is no longer accepting new memories. Pennyfarthing out!

I should have known to stop reading at "calendar girl," but somehow I soldiered on all the way to the second "Epstein." And I feel like I deserve a Nobel Prize in Medicine for reading that without aspirating to death on my own vomit.

But at least I know this story can't get any wor …

> "I've known Jeff for 15 years. Terrific guy," Mr. Trump told New York magazine in 2002. "He's a lot of fun to be with. It is even said that he likes beautiful women as much as I do, and many of them are on the younger side."

Jesus Fart-Gargling Christ, what the fuck is wrong with you?

Somehow you've made me miss those bygone, halcyon days when you merely *endorsed* pedophiles.

Ugh.

Love,
Pennyfarthing

July 10, 2019

- Before signing an executive order on kidney care, Trump says, "You've worked so hard on the kidney. Very special. The kidney has a very special place in the heart. It's an incredible thing."

From the Desk of Aldous J. Pennyfarthing
To: Donald Trump, feckless chucklefuck

Dear Pr*sident Assclown,

I know you're pretty obtuse, but wherever did you get the idea that airplane glue is something Dow Chemical invented for phlegmatic orange assholes to sniff on airplanes?

"The kidney has a very special place in the heart."

Oof.

Unless you're cribbing from a Jeff Dahmer cookbook — and it would *almost* be less frightening if you were — that is just another big, steaming bowl of *what-the-fuck?*

Every time you go off script it's like watching your preschool kid's bus driver take his hands off the wheel to do another bong hit. Just read the shit they put in front of you, okay, Patrick Horny? The only thing you ever add to your speeches is crushed red crazy pepper. No speechwriter anywhere wrote "the kidney has a very special place in the heart." Because that would be fucking impossible, as no one else on Earth is that stupid. Or ever has been, for that matter.

Jebus Crunchberries, I've seen squirrels with their heads stuck in Mountain Dew cans that were better prepared for this job than you.

Try cutting the Adderall with baking soda once in a while, 'k?

Love,
Pennyfarthing

◆ ◆ ◆

July 11, 2019

- At a White House social media summit, Trump whines about his Twitter follower count: "There's no doubt in my mind that I should have millions and millions — I have millions of people, so many people I wouldn't believe it — but I know we've been blocked. People come up to me and they say, 'Sir, I can't get you, I can't follow you. They make it impossible.' These are people who are really good at what they do. They say, 'They make it absolutely impossible.' And, you know, we can't have it."
- After excerpts of the book *American Carnage* reveal that former House Speaker Paul Ryan offered sharp criticism of Trump, Trump tweets, "Paul Ryan, the failed V.P. candidate & former Speaker of the House, whose record of achievement was atrocious (except during my first two years as President), ultimately became a long running lame duck failure, leaving his Party in the lurch both as a fundraiser & leader." The next day Trump says, "For him to be going out and opening his mouth is pretty incredible, but maybe he gets paid for that."

July 12, 2019

- Secretary of Labor Alex Acosta resigns in disgrace over accusations that he once gave a far too lenient plea deal to pedophile and Trump pal Jeffrey Epstein.

July 14, 2019

- Trump tweets, "So interesting to see 'Progressive' Democrat Congresswomen, who originally came from countries whose governments are a complete and total catastrophe, the worst, most corrupt and inept anywhere in the world (if they even have a functioning government at all), now loudly and viciously telling the people of the United States, the greatest and most powerful Nation on earth, how our government is to be run. Why don't they go back and help fix the totally broken and crime infested places from which they came. Then come back and show us how it is done. These places need your help badly, you can't leave fast enough. I'm sure that Nancy Pelosi would be very happy to quickly work out free travel arrangements!"

From the Desk of Aldous J. Pennyfarthing
To: Donald Trump, racist piss-weasel

Dear Pr*sident Assclown,

Okay, you're tweeting about Alexandria Ocasio-Cortez, Ayanna Pressley, Rashida Tlaib, and Ilhan Omar. All are women of color; all are U.S. citizens; only one is an immigrant.

So three of them came from America, which *isn't* broken and crime-infested, unless you're specifically talking about the White House.

So what about these four women would make you think of them as foreigners? Hmm, what could that be? I'm puzzled.

Now, both your paternal grandparents were from Germany. Your mother was from Scotland. And even though you recently claimed your father was born in Germany, he was actually born in New York.

You've previously said (including in *The Art of the Deal*) that your family was from Sweden.

So when World War II started, your German-born-not-German-born-but-definitely-ethnically-German father would have been 36 and living in the United States. By that time he had a pretty well-established real estate business.

Did anyone tell him to go back to the Nazi-infested country he originally came from?

Maybe, but I doubt it. Because 1) he kept telling everyone he was Swedish and 2) he was ... oh, here it is ... white.

Meanwhile, like you, Alexandria Ocasio-Cortez was born in New York to a (like you) American father and an (unlike you) native-born American (i.e., Puerto Rican) mother. And she's ... let's see ... oh, this is interesting ... Latina.

So I'm tempted to ask what just disgorged from your egregious, broke-ass H.R. Pufnstuf head, but you really don't know, do you?

You're like a racist septic tank. Sometimes you just overflow, and we simply have to deal with it until the stench goes away.

Love,
Pennyfarthing

July 15, 2019

- Trump tells White House counselor Kellyanne Conway to ignore a subpoena from the House Oversight Committee.
- The White House projects a $1 trillion deficit for 2019. While running for president, Trump had promised to eliminate the entire federal debt.
- In a bid to end protections for most Central American asylum seekers, the Trump administration enacts a rule that says immigrants passing through another country before arriving at the border must seek asylum there before being eligible for asylum in the U.S.

July 16, 2019

- Trump tweets, "'Billionaire Tech Investor Peter Thiel believes Google should be investigated for treason. He accuses Google of working with the Chinese Government.' @foxandfriends A great and brilliant guy who knows this subject better than anyone! The Trump Administration will take a look!"

July 17, 2019

- NBC News uncovers footage from 1992 of Trump partying with pedophile Jeffrey Epstein and patting a woman's behind.
- When a Rohingya refugee asks Trump how he will help the Rohingya refugees in Myanmar, Trump re-

plies, "Where is that exactly?"
- The House votes to hold Attorney General William Barr and Commerce Secretary Wilbur Ross in criminal contempt for refusing to comply with subpoenas related to Congress' investigation of the Trump administration's campaign to add a citizenship question to the 2020 census.
- During a rally in North Carolina, Trump supporters shout "send her back!" in reference to Rep. Ilhan Omar, a U.S. citizen whom Trump had earlier suggested should go back to "the totally broken and crime infested places from which [she] came." Trump basks in the chant for 13 seconds without giving any indication that he wants it to stop. The next day Trump claims he was "unhappy" with the chant and "started speaking very quickly" in order to nip it in the bud.

From the Desk of Aldous J. Pennyfarthing
To: Donald Trump, senile implant

Dear Pr*sident Assclown,

You are the TruckNutz of U.S. presidents.

Love,
Pennyfarthing

July 19, 2019

- In reference to the Democratic freshman congresswomen known as "The Squad" — Alexandria Ocasio-Cortez, Ilhan Omar, Ayanna Pressley, and Rashida Tlaib — Trump says, "They can't talk about 'evil Jews,' which is what they say: 'evil Jews.'" For the record, none of them has ever referred to "evil Jews."

July 21, 2019

- Trump tweets, "I don't believe the four Congresswomen are capable of loving our Country. They should apologize to America (and Israel) for the horrible (hateful) things they have said. They are destroying the Democrat Party, but are weak & insecure people who can never destroy our great Nation!"

July 22, 2019

- Trump tweets, "The 'Squad' is a very Racist group of troublemakers who are young, inexperienced, and not very smart. They are pulling the once great Democrat Party far left, and were against humanitarian aid at the Border. And are now against ICE and Homeland Security. So bad for our Country!"
- While discussing the war in Afghanistan, Trump says, "I could win that war in a week, I just don't want to kill 10 million people. … Afghanistan would be wiped off the face of the earth. It would be over in literally, in 10 days, and I don't want to go that route, so we're working with Pakistan and others to extricate ourselves."
- Politico reports that the Commerce Department is a dysfunctional "disaster" and that its secretary, Wilbur Ross, falls asleep during meetings.

From the Desk of Aldous J. Pennyfarthing
To: Donald Trump, Great Sphincter of Geezer

Dear Pr*sident Assclown,

How do you tell the difference between a wakeful and sleeping

Wilbur Ross? That's not the setup for a joke. I seriously want to know. He looks like Nosferatu's fetus, for fuck's sake.

Thanks again for hiring all the best people. I kind of wish they'd *all* fall asleep so the White House could be overtaken by feral cats. *I'd* sleep way better in meetings if the cats were in charge, I can tell you that.

So weird that something you're ultimately in charge of would be described as "dysfunctional," though. I mean, you only bankrupted a *few* casinos — which, granted, is the business equivalent of getting a beehive stuck on your head and falling naked down a manhole. But still. I can count them on one hand. Not too bad for a functional illiterate like you.

I guess as long as Ross doesn't insult your intelligence or backtalk you in some other way, he'll be fine. Eventually he'll die in his chair and they can carry him away in a beach pail. Or you could just keep his moldering, peanut-brittle-looking corpse around for another couple years. Like anyone would notice.

Love,
Pennyfarthing

◆ ◆ ◆

July 23, 2019

- Trump tweets, "Farmers are starting to do great again, after 15 years of a downward spiral. The 16 Billion Dollar China 'replacement' money didn't exactly hurt!"
- Speaking at Turning Point USA's Teen Student Action Summit, Trump says, "Those numbers in California and numerous other states, they're rigged. They've got people voting that shouldn't be voting. They vote many times, not just twice, not just three times. It's like a circle. They come back, they put a new hat on.

They come back, they put a new shirt on. And in many cases, they don't even do that. You know what's going on. It's a rigged deal." He also says, "Then, I have an Article II, where I have the right to do whatever I want as president. But I don't even talk about that."

From the Desk of Aldous J. Pennyfarthing
To: Donald Trump, 45 shades of shit

Dear Pr*sident Assclown,

This bears repeating:

> "Then, I have an Article II, where I have the right to do whatever I want as president. But I don't even talk about that."

First of all, if Article II of the Constitution really *did* allow you to do whatever you wanted, you'd be riding Mike Pence like a horsey through the Lincoln Memorial Reflecting Pool while wearing Steve Bannon's tenderly flayed hide as a ghillie suit. But ya can't, Gladys. Ya can't.

Secondly, you "don't even talk about that"? Uh. YOU SAID THAT A WEEK AGO IN YOUR INTERVIEW WITH GEORGE STEPHANOPOULOS, AND YOU'RE SAYING IT AGAIN NOW!

(Yeah, sorry about the capital letters. Sometimes I beat on my keyboard with my exuberantly bloody, ground chuck slab of a forehead and accidentally turn on the caps lock without noticing. Also, I'm not really sorry. Also, fuck you, mushroom dick.)

And this nonsense about people putting on new shirts and hats so they can vote multiple times? Exactly when did that gelastic turd of a fart-fable sprout gossamer wings and fly out of your ass? That simply doesn't happen. Oh, how do I know? Because I live in America and not in a Benny Hill sketch.

Also, studies have proven that in-person election fraud is about as rare as the minuscule coterie of brain cells in your head that somehow haven't been irretrievably besotted with Adderall and howler monkey sex hormones.

So just shut it, Eleanor. Umkay?

Thanks.

Love,
Pennyfarthing

◆ ◆ ◆

July 24, 2019

- Robert Mueller testifies before the House Judiciary and House Intelligence committees.
- Trump tweets, "Why didn't Robert Mueller & his band of 18 Angry Democrats spend any time investigating Crooked Hillary Clinton, Lyin' & Leakin' James Comey, Lisa Page and her Psycho lover, Peter S, Andy McCabe, the beautiful Ohr family, Fusion GPS, and many more, including HIMSELF & Andrew W?"
- Trump coins the words "infantroopen" and "lawmurkers" during a speech in Washington.

◆ ◆ ◆

July 25, 2019

- *The Washington Post* reports that Trump appeared in front of a fake presidential seal at the Turning Point USA Teen Student Action Summit. The phony seal featured an eagle with two heads grasping a set of golf clubs and a wad of cash. And instead of "E pluribus unum" the seal said "45 es un títere," which is Spanish for "45 is a puppet."

July 26, 2019

- In a 5-4 decision, the Supreme Court says Trump can put $2.5 billion in military funds toward construction of his wall along the southern border.

July 27, 2019

- Trump tweets, "Rep, Elijah Cummings has been a brutal bully, shouting and screaming at the great men & women of Border Patrol about conditions at the Southern Border, when actually his Baltimore district is FAR WORSE and more dangerous. His district is considered the Worst in the USA. As proven last week during a Congressional tour, the Border is clean, efficient & well run, just very crowded. Cumming [sic] District is a disgusting, rat and rodent infested mess. If he spent more time in Baltimore, maybe he could help clean up this very dangerous & filthy place."

From the Desk of Aldous J. Pennyfarthing
To: Donald Trump, Regina Gorged

Dear Pr*sident Assclown,

I see you haven't given up on Maryland's 10 electoral votes, huh? Way to represent every citizen. You're a real mensch.

So do you get up every morning thinking of new ways to embarrass the country and everyone in it, or does this racist piffle just spew from your head naturally like pus from a Gary Busey back zit?

What are you gonna do to top this one, Reich Minister? Maybe an executive order declaring that black people don't float? Question: When you ~~read about~~ heard about Joseph Goebbels in high school, did you understand that you were in a history class and not a job-training seminar? Because I don't think you came away with the right lesson. Just my 2 cents.

By the way, Elijah Cummings is a legend, whereas you're just a bellend.

Also, the failing/flailing real estate investor and poor man's Billy Carter who married your daughter Ivanka is *literally* a Baltimore slumlord. So maybe talk to him about the "mess" there, okay?

Love,
Pennyfarthing

July 28, 2019

- Trump announces that Director of National Intelligence Dan Coats will resign in August.

July 29, 2019

- During a signing ceremony for the 9/11 first responders bill, Trump jokes that the stage may not hold up, but if it does collapse "we're not falling very far." He also says, "I was down there also. But I'm not considering myself a first responder. But I was down there I spent a lot of time down there with you."

July 30, 2019

- North Korea tests missiles for the second time in less than a week. Trump later tweets, "Kim Jong Un and North Korea tested 3 short range missiles over the last number of days. These missiles tests are not a violation of our signed Singapore agreement, nor was there discussion of short range missiles when we shook hands. There may be a United Nations violation, but Chairman Kim does not want to disappoint me with a violation of trust, there is far too much for North Korea to gain - the potential as a Country, under Kim Jong Un's leadership, is unlimited. Also, there is far too much to lose. I may be wrong, but I believe that Chariman Kim has a great and beautiful vision for his country, and only the United States, with me as President, can make that vision come true. He will do the right thing because he is far too smart not to, and he does not want to disappoint his friend, President Trump!"
- Defending himself against accusations of racism in the wake of his tweets about Elijah Cummings and Baltimore, Trump says, "I am the least racist person there is anywhere in the world. ... What I've done for African Americans in two and a half years, no president has been able to do anything like it."

July 31, 2019

- Trump tweets, "If I hadn't won the 2016 Election, we would be in a Great Recession/Depression right now. The people I saw on stage last night, & you can add in Sleepy Joe, Harris, & the rest, will lead us into an economic sinkhole the likes of which we have

never seen before. With me, only up!"
- Trump offers Vladimir Putin help in battling large Siberian wildfires. In November 2018, he tweeted this: "There is no reason for these massive, deadly and costly forest fires in California except that forest management is so poor. Billions of dollars are given each year, with so many lives lost, all because of gross mismanagement of the forests. Remedy now, or no more Fed payments!"

From the Desk of Aldous J. Pennyfarthing
To: Donald Trump, Crisco inferno

Dear Pr*sident Assclown,

America first! Except for the people who didn't vote for you! Fuck them!

Good God, man. If you gave me a particle accelerator and Fermilab's super-secret juju for creating wormholes, I couldn't get farther up Putin's ass than you are right now.

I know you suck at geography, but California is one of our states. Sure, it's bluer than your balls during one of your couples retreats with Melania, but presidents are supposed to represent *all* U.S. citizens. You've formed a clique that hates all the nerds and drama kids, and worse, you want to shove us all into lockers for at least another year.

It's nice of you to want to help the guy who got you elected, but we have priorities in this country. One of those is not letting half of our most populous state burn to the ground because no one there likes you.

Love,
Pennyfarthing

August 2, 2019

- Just days after being nominated, Rep. John Ratcliffe withdraws from consideration as Trump's director of national intelligence. Trump tweets that Ratcliffe has been "treated very unfairly by the LameStream Media."
- Trump claims that the mainstream media, which he has frequently dismissed as "fake news," helps his administration vet his nominees: "I get a name, I give it out to the press and you vet for me. A lot of time you do a very good job. Not always. If you look at the vetting process for the White House, it is very good, but you are part of the vetting process. I give out a name to the press and you vet for me, we save a lot of money that way."
- Trump sarcastically tweets, "Really bad news! The Baltimore house of Elijah Cummings was robbed. Too bad!"

August 3, 2019

- Twenty-two people are killed during a mass shooting in El Paso. Echoing Trump's own racist rhetoric, the killer's manifesto warns of a "Hispanic invasion" of Texas.
- Fourteen minutes after tweeting about the horrific mass shooting in El Paso, Trump tweets his well-wishes to UFC fighter Colby Covington: "Fight hard tonight Colby," he writes. "You are a real Champ! #MAGA"
- The same day of the deadly El Paso mass shooting, Trump is photographed partying at his New Jersey golf club.

From the Desk of Aldous J. Pennyfarthing
To: Donald Trump, slubberdegullion

Dear Pr*sident Assclown,

They say the amygdala is the nutsack of the brain, and I feel like I've been kicked there repeatedly — i.e., *every goddamn day* — for at least the past two years.

Okay, no one actually says that except me, but I think it fits.

Here's a brief description of the amygdala, from Science Daily:

> The amygdala (Latin, corpus amygdaloideum) is an almond-shaped set of neurons located deep in the brain's medial temporal lobe.
>
> Shown to play a key role in the processing of emotions, the amygdala forms part of the limbic system.
>
> In humans and other animals, this subcortical brain structure is linked to both fear responses and pleasure.
>
> Its size is positively correlated with aggressive behavior across species.
>
> ...
>
> Conditions such as anxiety, autism, depression, post-traumatic stress disorder, and phobias are suspected of being linked to abnormal functioning of the amygdala, owing to damage, developmental problems, or neurotransmitter imbalance.

That's a lot of abstruse scientific argot that really just boils down to "stop fucking kicking me in my brain-nuts, Trump!"

Anyway, what was my point?

Oh, yeah. You partied on the night of yet another mass shooting. Because you're you.

Oh, and 14 minutes after sending out a "condolence" tweet, you tweeted well-wishes to a UFC fighter. Because life goes on, I guess. Huh?

Except you're supposedly president, and it's the president's job to … ah, fuck it. You don't care.

Love,
Pennyfarthing

August 4, 2019

- An early-morning mass shooting in Dayton, Ohio, leaves nine dead.
- Following mass shootings in El Paso and Dayton, Trump says, "We have done much more than most administrations [on the issue]. That's not talked about very much. But we've done actually a lot. But perhaps more has to be done."

August 5, 2019

- In a speech following the massacres in El Paso and Dayton, Trump blames white supremacy, video games, mental illness, and the internet for the violence. He neglects to mention his own racist rhetoric.

August 6, 2019

- Trump tweets, "As they have learned in the last two

years, our great American Farmers know that China will not be able to hurt them in that their President has stood with them and done what no other president would do - And I'll do it again next year if necessary!"

August 7, 2019

- Trump tweets, "Watching Sleepy Joe Biden making a speech. Sooo Boring! The LameStream Media will die in the ratings and clicks with this guy. It will be over for them, not to mention the fact that our Country will do poorly with him. It will be one big crash, but at least China will be happy!"

August 8, 2019

- A new Pentagon report concludes that ISIS is "resurging" in Syria after Trump declared it had been "100 percent defeated."
- Reports emerge that the Trump administration called two victims of the El Paso shooting back to the hospital so Trump could be photographed with them. One of these was a 2-month-old orphan who was shielded by his parents during the shooting. None of the eight patients who were at the hospital during Trump's visit wanted to meet with the pr*sident.
- Video surfaces showing Trump bragging about his crowd sizes as he attempts to console victims of a mass shooting in El Paso: "That was some crowd. We had twice the number outside. And

then you had this crazy Beto [O'Rourke]. Beto had like 400 people in a parking lot, and they said his crowd was wonderful." *The Washington Post* reports that Trump "complain[ed] loudly on Air Force One, wanted pictures and video released immediately, according to people with knowledge of what happened, and asked aides to defend him. Trump has complained to allies since the shooting that he has not gotten enough credit for his response, according to these people, who spoke on the condition of anonymity to share private conversations."

From the Desk of Aldous J. Pennyfarthing
To: Donald Trump, gross, pointless blank

Dear Pr*sident Assclown,

Holy fuck.

There's simply not enough vomit in the world to properly respond to this.

So after two mass shootings — one of which appeared to be inspired by your own hateful rhetoric — you 1) went dancing, 2) wished a UFC fighter good luck in his upcoming bout, 3) forced a child whose parents were killed in one of the shootings to return to the hospital for a photo op, 4) bragged about your crowd sizes compared to those of a Democratic presidential candidate, and 5) loudly complained to your staff that you weren't getting enough credit for your "compassionate" response.

And nice job with that photo op, dude. You and Melania standing there with pasted-on smiles, you flashing a thumbs-up with your vanishingly small pinto bean of a digit, while the newly orphaned baby gapes unwittingly into an uncertain future of your own creation — it was a *tour de force*.

Well done, Kodos. You've got the alien-reptile demographic salted away, that's for sure. Bit of advice? Maybe keep that photo away from anything warm-blooded. It could make a Civil War triage surgeon vomit his small intestines.

You'd think someone who's allegedly been human for 73 years would have picked up at least a few human tics — by osmosis, if nothing else. I guess pop culture has trained me to expect psychopaths to be brilliant at concealing their utter lack of empathy. But you're not Hannibal Lecter so much as John Wayne Gacy with extra clown makeup. That photo would give Ted Cruz the creeps, FFS.

Good luck in your lifetime quest to become a real boy. It could happen. You never know.

Love,
Pennyfarthing

August 9, 2019

- Trump uses a mock Asian accent while imitating South Korean President Moon Jae-in during a big-money fundraiser in the Hamptons.

August 10, 2019

- Trump tweets, "In a letter to me sent by Kim Jong Un, he stated, very nicely, that he would like to meet and start negotiations as soon as the joint U.S./South Korea joint exercise are over. It was a long letter, much of it complaining about the ridiculous and expensive exercises. It was also a small apology for testing the short range missiles, and that this testing would stop when the exercises end. I look forward to seeing Kim Jong Un in the not too distant future! A nuclear free

North Korea will lead to one of the most successful countries in the world!"
- Trump retweets a conspiracy theory suggesting Bill Clinton killed Jeffrey Epstein in prison.

From the Desk of Aldous J. Pennyfarthing
To: Donald Trump, diseased meatsicle

Dear Pr*sident Assclown,

All right you gelatinous fuck. Listen up now.

Now who was BFFs with (confirmed pedophile) Jeffrey Epstein?

Who currently has access to the levers of control in government?

Who would like to see the Jeffrey Epstein sex abuse story buried deeper than the wobbly hunk of rebar in Jared Kushner's head?

That's right. YOU, motherfucker.

So how does shit like this happen?

NBC News:

> President Donald Trump retweeted a conspiracy theory Saturday evening alleging without evidence that former President Bill Clinton was connected to the death of wealthy financier and accused sex trafficker Jeffrey Epstein, hours after Epstein was found dead by apparent suicide in his federal prison cell.
>
> "Died of SUICIDE on 24/7 SUICIDE WATCH ? Yeah right! How does that happen," Terrence K. Williams, a conservative commentator and comedian, wrote in the message retweeted by Trump. In a two-minute-long selfie video recording, Williams alleged that the Clintons were responsible for Epstein's death.

Okay, so Epstein wasn't on suicide watch at the time. That's thing one. Secondly, none of the conspiracy theories you believe are even remotely true, except for your nagging suspicion that Melania is hoping you'll scratch your face in *juuuuussttt* the right spot one day and your head will burst open like a piñata. That one — or at least some version of it — is definitely true.

But, no, the Clintons didn't murder Jeffrey Epstein *or* Vince Foster, Barack Obama wasn't born in Kenya, Antonin Scalia wasn't murdered with a pillow, exercise isn't bad for you, and millions of people didn't illegally cast votes for Hillary in 2016.

Also, Batboy isn't real, ancient astronauts didn't build the pyramids at Giza, the moon landing actually happened, the Earth is not flat, QAnon isn't a real thing, vaccines don't cause autism, long red ties don't make portly Oompa-Loompas look thin, and that wall will get built sometime after your son Eric generates an Einstein-Rosen bridge to Betelgeuse by farting in the tub with a Millennium Falcon up his ass.

But the pee tape? Oh, yeah, I absolutely believe *that* exists.

Love,
Pennyfarthing

August 11, 2019

- Trump tweets, "Scaramucci, who like so many others had nothing to do with my Election victory, is only upset that I didn't want him back in the Administration (where he desperately wanted to be). Also, I seldom had time to return his many calls to me. He just wanted to be on TV!"
- *The New York Times* reports that the Department of Homeland Security is being handcuffed by Trump's

lack of interest in domestic terrorism and white supremacist violence.

August 13, 2019

- During a visit to a Shell plant in Pennsylvania, Trump complains that the presidency is costing him billions of dollars: "This thing is costing me a fortune, being president. Somebody said, 'Oh, he might have rented a room to a man from Saudi Arabia for $500.' What about the $5 billion that I'll lose? You know, it's probably gonna cost me, including upside, downside, lawyers, because every day they sue me for something. These are the most litigious people. It's probably costing me from $3 to $5 billion for the privilege of being — and I couldn't care less, I don't care."

August 14, 2019

- The Trump administration proposes a rule allowing federal contractors to "make employment decisions consistent with their sincerely held religious tenets and beliefs without fear of sanction by the federal government." Critics warn that the rule would allow companies to discriminate against LGBTQ people.
- A petition to rename a portion of Manhattan's Fifth Avenue — specifically the stretch in front of Trump Tower — President Barack H. Obama Avenue attracts hundreds of thousands of signatures.

From the Desk of Aldous J. Pennyfarthing
To: Donald Trump, churl in charge

Dear Pr*sident Assclown,

Oh, please, please, please, please, please, please, please, please, *please* let this happen. If every piece of mail you got had Barack Obama's name on it, you would literally shit your spleen out your navel.

I haven't willingly consumed meat in 27 years, but I would eat a live hyena's asshole if it helped make this happen.

I would saw off my own face with dental tape.

I would caramelize my nipples with a welder's torch like a pair of mini crème brûlées.

I would shave my head, chest, and taint with a conch shell, fill a bathtub with Sriracha, and soak in it for a fortnight. (Or however long it might take.)

I would let Carrot Top ravage me with his choice of comedy prop.

This *has* to happen. Something good has to come of the Kafkaesque bowl of olid Spaghettios and baby seal tears that is your presidency.

In fact, if the street in front of your garish tower is named after Barack Obama, you'll likely get lots of mail from well-wishers. Assuming you're not in prison. But, hey, we could rename the street in front of Sing Sing, too. How does Adam Schiff Way sound?

Love,
Pennyfarthing

August 15, 2019

- Demonstrating that he knows nothing about the glo-

- bal economy, Trump tweets, "The United States is now, by far, the Biggest, Strongest and Most Powerful Economy in the World, it is not even close! As others falter, we will only get stronger. Consumers are in the best shape ever, plenty of cash. Business Optimism is at an All Time High!"
- Trump tweets, "It would show great weakness if Israel allowed Rep. Omar and Rep.Tlaib to visit. They hate Israel & all Jewish people, & there is nothing that can be said or done to change their minds. Minnesota and Michigan will have a hard time putting them back in office. They are a disgrace!"
- At a rally in New Hampshire, Trump mocks an audience member's appearance: "That guy's got a serious weight problem. Go home, start exercising." It's later revealed that the rallygoer is a Trump supporter. Trump also claims he was once named Michigan's "Man of the Year," though it remains unclear to all living sentient beings what he's talking about.

From the Desk of Aldous J. Pennyfarthing
To: Donald Trump, one-eyed web slinger

Dear Pr*sident Assclown,

"That guy's got a serious weight problem. Go home, start exercising."

Wow.

That's like the potbelly calling the bushpig fat.

And could there ever be a more perfect demonstration of the absolute sway you hold over your cult? You called one of your fans a gross tub of lard, and he STILL SUPPORTS YOU.

I think I may start calling you Jim "Big Boned" Jones.

Also, you've never been named Michigan's "Man of the Year."

That's just made up, and you know it. Take it from a four-time Pulitzer Prize-winning author and Nobel laureate.

Love,
Pennyfarthing

❖ ❖ ❖

August 16, 2019

- After Trump makes more unfounded claims about fraudulent voting during the 2016 election, FEC Chair Ellen Weintraub releases a statement demanding he supply proof of his allegations.
- Reports surface that Trump has more than once discussed buying Greenland. Trump later cancels a planned visit to Denmark after its prime minister says Greenland isn't for sale: "Denmark is a very special country with incredible people, but based on Prime Minister Mette Frederiksen's comments, that she would have no interest in discussing the purchase of Greenland, I will be postponing our meeting scheduled in two weeks for another time. The Prime Minister was able to save a great deal of expense and effort for both the United States and Denmark by being so direct. I thank her for that and look forward to rescheduling sometime in the future!"

From the Desk of Aldous J. Pennyfarthing
To: Donald Trump, tinyfist destiny

Dear Pr*sident Assclown,

Hmm, looks like someone just watched the "Schoolhouse Rock" episode about the Louisiana Purchase.

So even if the polar ice caps don't melt, I anticipate our coastal cities will be underwater in another two years from all the spit-takes their residents do after reading about the stupid shit you've said.

Oh, but Greenland's ice sheets are eroding faster than a bargain bin butt plug in Mike Pence's rectum.

I can only assume you want to buy it because you saw the original *Superman* movie. If you were president of Greenland, you could sit on the ice sheets in your tuxedo (passing yourself off as either an emperor penguin with gigantism or a 90-gallon Hefty Bag overflowing with clown pubes and hay), melt the ever-living fuck out of them, and turn all your inland property into valuable beachfront sites for condos.

Or else it still irks you that none of the 50 states in our venerable union are named Trumptopia. So you need to create your own state. One that has free universal health care and a burgeoning sustainable-energy economy that you'll instantly replace with coal plants, Chick-fil-A restaurants, and systemic racism.

Okay, so that's all well and good. You want to buy Greenland. Weird thought, but whatever.

Then this happened:

> "Greenland is not for sale. I strongly hope that this is not meant seriously." — Denmark Prime Minister Mette Frederiksen

And this.

From NPR:

> President Trump has called the Danish prime minister's comments "nasty" after she rejected the idea of selling Greenland to the United States as "absurd" — in an escalation of diplomatic tensions that began suddenly last week.
>
> Trump complained Wednesday at the White House

that Danish Prime Minister Mette Frederiksen's statement was "not nice" and showed disrespect.

"All she had to do was say 'No, we wouldn't be interested,'" he told reporters. "She's not talking to me, she's talking to the United States of America."

The president announced in a Tuesday night tweet that he was calling off his visit to Denmark.

Okay, a sovereign country thinks the idea of selling you Greenland is ridiculous so you take your pendulous, scurfy, STD-denuded balls and go home?

And, no, Frederiksen is not "talking to the United States of America." She's talking to a fluorescent orange peach-glazed ham with delusions of grandeur. Not remotely the same thing.

Love,
Pennyfarthing

August 18, 2019

- After Fox News releases a poll unfavorable to Trump, he says, "There's something going on at Fox, I'll tell you right now. And I'm not happy with it."
- The perpetually wrong Larry Kudlow, one of Trump's top economic advisers, tells *Meet the Press*' Chuck Todd, "I sure don't see a recession."

From the Desk of Aldous J. Pennyfarthing
To: Donald Trump, Tariff Man

Dear Pr*sident Assclown,

On a good day, listening to Larry Kudlow discuss economics is like watching the chief herpetologist at the Bronx Zoo run around screaming in the gift shop with a Gaboon viper latched to his scrotum. So, naturally, you made him your top economic adviser.

"I sure don't see a recession." — Larry Kudlow

"I sure don't see an iceberg." — Edward Smith, captain of the Titanic

Okay, we'll see, Nostra-dumbass.

Of course, Kudlow has been wrong before. Like really, really, really, really, really, *really* fucking wrong.

Here he was in a December 2007 *National Review* column that, remarkably, is still available online:

> There is no recession. Despite all the doom and gloom from the economic pessimistas, the resilient U.S economy continues moving ahead "quarter after quarter, year after year" defying dire forecasts and delivering positive growth. In fact, we are about to enter the seventh consecutive year of the Bush boom.
>
> …
>
> Earlier today, a doom and gloom economic forecast from Macro Economic Advisors was released predicting zero percent growth in the fourth quarter. This report is off by at least two percentage points. These guys are going to wind up with egg on their faces.

So not only did Kudlow end up with egg on *his* face, he was baked into an omelet and served feet first to angry beavers. And yet he's your *top economic adviser*.

Holy shit, you're — and I can't stress this nearly enough — a fucking idiot.

Say, during your interview, did you ask him how his Pets.com stock was doing? I'm understandably curious.

When you're no longer president and you continue on in the shadows as Tariff Man, will Kudlow still be your sidekick?

I can't wait. Truly. I'll start sewing your cape now. Let me guess. XXXXXXL?

Love,
Pennyfarthing

August 19, 2019

- Trump tweets, "Anthony Scaramucci is a highly unstable 'nut job' who was with other candidates in the primary who got shellaced, and then unfortunately wheedled his way into my campaign. I barely knew him until his 11 days of gross incompetence-made a fool of himself, bad on TV. Abused staff ... got fired."

August 20, 2019

- Trump says, "I think any Jewish people that vote for a Democrat, I think it shows either a total lack of knowledge or great disloyalty." According to Pew Research, 79 percent of Jews voted for Democrats during the 2018 midterms.
- After hearing from the NRA, Trump backs away from gun-control measures he appeared to endorse in the wake of mass shootings in El Paso and Dayton: "The people that — a lot of the people that put me where I am, are strong believers in the Second Amendment, and I am also. And we have to be very careful about that. You know, they call it the slippery slope."
- Trump again defends Vladimir Putin, saying, "I could

certainly see it being the G8 again. As you know, for most of the time it was the G8 and it included Russia. And President Obama didn't want Russia in because he got outsmarted. Well, that's not really the way it should work."

August 21, 2019

- On Twitter, Trump quotes weirdo conspiracy theorist Wayne Allyn Root, who says Israelis love Trump like he's "the second coming of God" and the "King of Israel."
- While talking to reporters, Trump says, "This isn't my trade war, this is a trade war that should have taken place a long time ago. Somebody had to do it." Then, looking to the sky, he says, "I am the chosen one."
- Asked what survivors of mass shootings want in terms of gun laws, Trump says, "Not only did they meet with me, they were pouring out of the room. The doctors were coming out of the operating rooms. There were hundreds and hundreds of people all over the floor. You couldn't even walk on it."

From the Desk of Aldous J. Pennyfarthing
To: Donald Trump, roly-poly Moses

Dear Pr*sident Assclown,

Christ.

You know, I used to like getting up in the morning, pouring a piping hot mug of coffee, and reading the news. But for the past two and a half years every burgeoning new dawn has felt like waking up from an Elysian dream and instantly getting my dick slammed in a leather-bound copy of the DSM-V.

You have lost your wee little mind, Caligu-lard.

Let's check out that barmy-as-batshit Wayne Allyn Root quote you tweeted out:

> "President Trump is the greatest President for Jews and for Israel in the history of the world, not just America, he is the best President for Israel in the history of the world and the Jewish people in Israel love him like he's the King of Israel. They love him like he is the second coming of God. But American Jews don't know him or like him. They don't even know what they're doing or saying anymore. It makes no sense! But that's OK, if he keeps doing what he's doing, he's good for all Jews, Blacks, Gays, everyone. And importantly, he's good for everyone in America who wants a job."

Oh, and the day before that you said this:

> "I think any Jewish people that vote for a Democrat, I think it shows either a total lack of knowledge or great disloyalty."

Okay, sure. You do realize that, like, 80 percent of American Jews are Democrats, right? That's four out of five. Here's how you remember that: It's the same number of cake slices you eat when you, Melania, and Barron celebrate Barron's birthday each year.

And you're the chosen one? Dude, I could take a shit out of any window in Nebraska and hit a better president.

But this is my favorite:

> "Not only did they meet with me, they were pouring out of the room. The doctors were coming out of the operating rooms. There were hundreds and hundreds of people all over the floor. You couldn't even walk

on it."

Mmm-hmm. Doctors were coming out of operating rooms to meet with you. I can only speak for myself, but if I'm elbows deep in throbbing arteries and viscera, I'm not interrupting my work to step into the lobby to gaze upon your beatific visage — which, let's face it, is pretty much a lateral move from staring at half-sutured guts.

So, yeah, that just didn't happen. No surgeons were leaving patients to die on the operating table because they were ineluctably drawn to your siren call. And I'm not even going to look this up on PolitiFact, because it's fucking impossible.

Love,
Pennyfarthing

August 22, 2019

- A former White House official tells *The New York Times* that Trump once joked about trading Puerto Rico for Greenland.

August 23, 2019

- Trump tweets, "Our great American companies are hereby ordered to immediately start looking for an alternative to China, including bringing your companies HOME and making your products in the USA. I will be responding to China's Tariffs this afternoon. This is a GREAT opportunity for the United States."
- The Trump administration files an amicus brief asking the Supreme Court to allow businesses to fire workers based on their sexual orientation.

- Trump tweets, "My only question is, who is our bigger enemy, Jay Powel [sic] or Chairman Xi?"
- In "honor" of two U.S. soldiers killed in Afghanistan, Trump tweets, "Highest Condolences!"

From the Desk of Aldous J. Pennyfarthing
To: Donald Trump, close encounter of the derp kind

Dear Pr*sident Assclown,

You've done it again, Kodos.

"Highest condolences from the Supreme Regent of Altair IV to the symbiotic podmates of the fallen Earthli ... er, *brave American soldiers!*"

But you're not an alien! Repeat. NOT an alien.

Definitely not.

Then again, if this were a movie, there'd be a scene at the end where hundreds of fat, orange proto-torsos in various stages of larval development were found floating in viscous-fluid chambers deep inside a bunker under Irkutsk, Siberia.

Oh, but it's not a movie.

Is it?

Love,
Pennyfarthing

◆ ◆ ◆

August 24, 2019

- Trump tweets, "The Media is destroying the Free Press! Mark Levin. So True!"

◆ ◆ ◆

August 25, 2019

- *The New York Times* reports that "a loose network of conservative operatives allied with the White House is pursuing what they say will be an aggressive operation to discredit news organizations deemed hostile to President Trump by publicizing damaging information about journalists."
- While at the G7 summit, Trump tweets, "The question I was asked most today by fellow World Leaders, who think the USA is doing so well and is stronger than ever before, happens to be, "Mr. President, why does the American media hate your Country so much? Why are they rooting for it to fail?"
- When asked whether he has second thoughts about his trade war with China, Trump says, "Yeah, sure. Why not?" When pressed further, he says, "Might as well. Might as well." Asked again, he responds, "I have second thoughts about everything."
- Axios reports that Trump, on multiple occasions, suggested using nuclear weapons to disrupt hurricanes that were heading to the U.S.

From the Desk of Aldous J. Pennyfarthing
To: Donald Trump, shartnado

Dear Pr*sident Assclown,

I've been in office brainstorming meetings where the manager said there's no such thing as a stupid question. Needless to say, you weren't in any of those meetings.

From Axios:

> President Trump has suggested multiple times to senior Homeland Security and national security officials that they explore using nuclear bombs to stop hurricanes from hitting the United States, according

to sources who have heard the president's private remarks and been briefed on a National Security Council memorandum that recorded those comments.

How is this real? I mean, how is this a real thing happening in the real world? Karl, you can turn off the simulation now! Not funny anymore! Karl! Karl!

My brother Karl has been known to play pranks on me. Once he sent a fake notice in to our Catholic high school's alumni newsletter saying I'd opened a new Christian bookstore called The Glory Hole to supplement my income from my busboy job at Dirty Sanchez's and my vacuum cleaner sales gig with Cleveland Steamers. He's gross and an awful human being, but I never thought he'd go this far.

Karl!

Knock it off!

Anyway, nukes to stop hurricanes. Sure, let's try it. Why not? I can't even imagine how that could backfire. That's a great plan, Donald. That's fucking ingenious, if I understand it correctly. It's a Swiss fucking watch.

I mean, before you dazzled me on the daily with your otherworldly intellect, I would have said that's the stupidest fucking thing I've ever heard. Dumber than putting you and your elephantine moobs on a Wheaties box. Dumber than licking a urinal cake at a Green Bay Arby's. Dumber than eating a McRib sandwich you found at the bottom of a McDonald's Playland ball pit. Dumber than voting for a reality star not named Snooki or The Situation.

But you're president, right? You must know something I don't.

So nukes it is!

Fire up that mothafuckin' nuke machine, dude! No more hurricanes EVAH!

Thank you, stable genius. You've saved us all.

Love,
Pennyfarthing

August 26, 2019

- At the G7 summit, Trump says, "I think I know more about the environment than most people." He also skips a discussion on climate change with other world leaders.
- Trump says he wants to hold the next G7 summit at his own Doral golf resort. Reports almost immediately surface that Doral has had troubles in the past with bedbugs.
- Trump says, "The first lady has gotten to know Kim Jong Un and I think she'd agree with me, he is a man with a country that has tremendous potential." The White House later confirms that Melania and Kim have never met.

From the Desk of Aldous J. Pennyfarthing
To: Donald Trump, oaf in office

Dear Pr*sident Assclown,

Hoo-boy. Lots of crazy to unpack today.

So the only way it makes sense to say Melania has gotten to know Kim Jong Un — given that she's never met him — is that you and Kim are essentially the same person.

And, hey, you *are!* If you were thinner and just a skosh more murderous, you'd be him.

Oh, but you're *not* him. Not exactly.

He's evil incarnate and you're evil in cling peach syrup.

He inherited a dysfunctional tyrannical state and you're a *self-made* madman.

He's a relatively swarthy Asian and you look like a bleached fart in a suit.

Other than that? Samesies.

Oh, and you're both trying to run kleptocracies. But for some reason those tedious "good government" people keep trying to stop you. He doesn't have these irksome problems.

Will it never end, this impudence?

Love,
Pennyfarthing

August 27, 2019

- *The Washington Post* reports that Trump has instructed Ag Secretary Sonny Perdue to exempt Alaska's Tongass National Forest from restrictions on logging.
- In a tweet, Trump appears to claim he's never heard of Axios, which broke the story about his wanting to kill hurricanes with nukes. He'd sat down for a lengthy interview with the news outlet months earlier.
- *The Washington Post* reports that Trump is so eager to build his southern border wall he's told subordinates he'll pardon them if they have to break any laws to get it built.
- Trump tweets, "No bedbugs at Doral. The Radical Left Democrats, upon hearing that the perfectly located (for the next G-7) Doral National MIAMI was under

consideration for the next G-7, spread that false and nasty rumor. Not nice!"

August 28, 2019

- Trump tweets, "We are tracking closely tropical storm Dorian as it heads, as usual, to Puerto Rico. FEMA and all others are ready, and will do a great job. When they do, let them know it, and give them a big Thank You - Not like last time. That includes from the incompetent Mayor of San Juan!"
- Trump aides admit that Trump fibbed about calls with China in order to boost the stock market. CNN: "Still, Trump flashed signs of optimism this week that the trade war could be resolved, saying he's received calls from Chinese officials saying they wanted to restart talks. Though Trump and Treasury Secretary Steven Mnuchin insisted there had been 'communication,' aides privately conceded the phone calls Trump described didn't happen the way he said they did. Instead, two officials said Trump was eager to project optimism that might boost markets, and conflated comments from China's vice premier with direct communication from the Chinese."

From the Desk of Aldous J. Pennyfarthing
To: Donald Trump, moral derp-itude

Dear Pr*sident Assclown,

You know, if you were a less scrupulous and moral man — bwah ha ha ha ha ha ha ha ha ha ha ha ha ha ha ha ha ha!

Sorry.

Wipes away tear

Less moral. Whoo! We both know that's impossible, right? I mean, if you broke out the family Ouija board and invited a legion of demons to possess your body, they'd immediately jump out of there like it was a hot tub with a turd floating in it.

Anyway, if you *were* a less moral man... sorry. One sec. Sorry.

Whoo!

Okay, I'm back.

If you were a less moral man, I could see you instructing proxies to buy up stock on your behalf or to short the market, and then when you jerked the market around with your grody little Vienna sausage tweetering fingers, you'd "earn" yourself quite a windfall. It would be *so* easy dude. A below-average child could do it, which is why I'm convinced this is exactly what you're up to.

To be clear, I have no evidence, much less proof, that you're doing this — other than the fact that you're you. Greedy, immoral, criminal, unscrupulous, unembraceable you.

I mean, I suppose it's a good thing to "boost" markets, but if the Dow gains on bullshit news, ultimately the people who bought in based on your word are going to get fucked sideways with your flaccid, ferociously fungal phallus. And if you happen to be manipulating the market for your own gain like I suspect you might be, you'd be *stealing* from them.

But then you're kind of a solipsist, right? Everyone in your world is just an object to be manipulated.

Tell me I'm wrong ... and then I'll tell *you* you're a bullshit-larded piñata just waiting to burst.

Love,
Pennyfarthing

August 29, 2019

- Trump officially establishes the U.S. military's Space Command.
- Following Trump's performance at the G7 summit, Business Insider interviews several current and former U.S. spies who say Trump is either a Russian asset or Putin's "useful idiot."
- Several media outlets report the Trump administration is rescinding permission for immigrants — including kids with cancer — to stay in the country while they undergo treatment for their illnesses. Sen Ed. Markey (D-Mass.), responds, "This is a new low even for Donald Trump."

From the Desk of Aldous J. Pennyfarthing
To: Donald Trump, sick fuck

Dear Pr*sident Assclown,

My mom used to say, "If you make that face for too long, it'll stick like that." I think a lot of our mothers said that, or something similar. It's a well-worn bromide. I always assumed it was just a bit of playful hyperbole.

Until now.

Now I'm actually worried, because for the past two and a half years my face perpetually looks as if I just found out about My Little Pony porn.

And, you know, appalling shit like deporting children with fucking *cancer* sure as fuck ain't helping matters.

I mean, you *are* the guy who tried to take health insurance away from your seriously ill grandnephew, but that's just one kid ... whom you're, uh, related to.

But these are just *strangers*' children ... with, uh, cancer or something.

Fuck me sideways with Rudy Giuliani's masticated elk jerky schlonger. This is some grotesquely evil, monstrous, Nazi-wannabe bullshit. I would never wish cancer on anyone, but I do hope your dick gets bitten off by a dyspeptic marsupial of God's choosing.

Love,
Pennyfarthing

❖ ❖ ❖

August 30, 2019

- Politico reports that Trump fired his personal assistant, Madeleine Westerhout, after she said Trump doesn't like to be in photos with his daughter Tiffany because he thinks she's overweight.
- Trump tweets out an image that appears to have been classified.

From the Desk of Aldous J. Pennyfarthing
To: Donald Trump, golden idler

Dear Pr*sident Assclown,

News item:

Donald Trump tweets out an aerial image of an Iranian rocket launchpad. *The Washington Post* interviews experts who say the image was "almost certainly highly classified."

MAGA moron response:

BUT HER EMAILS! BUT HER EMAILS! BUT HER EMAILS! BUT HER EMAILS! BUT HER EMAILS! BUT HER EMAILS! BUT HER EMAILS! BUT HER EMAILS! BUT HER EMAILS! BUT HER EMAILS! BUT HER EMAILS! BUT HER EMAILS! BUT HER EMAILS! BUT HER EMAILS! BUT HER EMAILS! BUT HER EMAILS! BUT HER

EMAILS! BUT HER EMAILS! BUT HER EMAILS! BUT HER EMAILS! BUT HER EMAILS! BUT HER EMAILS! BUT HER EMAILS! BUT HER EMAILS! BUT HER EMAILS! BUT HER EMAILS! BUT HER EMAILS! BUT HER EMAILS! BUT HER EMAILS! BUT HER EMAILS! BUT HER EMAILS! BUT HER EMAILS! BUT HER EMAILS! BUT HER EMAILS! BUT HER EMAILS!

Q.E.D.

Love,
Pennyfarthing

❖ ❖ ❖

August 31, 2019

- Trump tweets, "Has anyone noticed that the top shows on @foxnews and cable ratings are those that are Fair (or great) to your favorite President, me! Congratulations to @seanhannity for being the number one shoe [sic] on Cable Television!"
- In a new memoir, incoming Smithsonian Secretary Lonnie G. Bunch III reveals that, during Trump's visit to the National Museum of African American History and Culture, the new pr*sident didn't want to see anything "difficult." Bunch also writes, "The president paused in front of the exhibit that discussed the role of the Dutch in the slave trade. As he pondered the label I felt that maybe he was paying attention to the work of the museum. He quickly proved me wrong. As he turned from the display he said to me, 'You know, they love me in the Netherlands.' All I could say was let's continue walking."

From the Desk of Aldous J. Pennyfarthing
To: Donald Trump, Dutch cheat

Dear Pr*sident Assclown,

Finally! You got it! "You know, they love me in the Netherlands" is exactly the response we were looking for!

Cue balloons and confetti!

Charlie, you've won! You did it! You did it! I knew you would, I just knew you would!

I mean, who *wouldn't* tell a crazy lie about one's own popularity with the Dutch after witnessing the bleakest possible reminders of our nation's greatest shame — a shame that continues to haunt us to this day? That's *exactly* the correct response for a new president!

I misjudged you. I thought you sucked balls. How wrong I was.

Love,
Pennyfarthing

P.S. You're giving Sean Hannity too much credit when you call him a "shoe." He's far lower to the ground than that.

September 1, 2019

- When asked whether he has a message for Poland on the 80th anniversary of its invasion by Nazis, Trump says, "I just want to congratulate Poland. It's a great country with great people."
- As Hurricane Dorian threatens the U.S., Trump says, "I'm not sure that I've ever even heard of a Category 5."
- As Hurricane Dorian continues to close in on the U.S., Trump picks a Twitter fight with actress Debra Messing: "I have not forgotten that when it was announced that I was going to do The Apprentice, and when it then became a big hit, helping NBC's failed lineup greatly, @DebraMessing came up to me at an Upfront

- & profusely thanked me, even calling me 'Sir.' How times have changed!"
- After Trump tweets that Alabama may be in the path of Hurricane Dorian, the National Weather Service's Birmingham station tweets, "Alabama will NOT see any impacts from #Dorian. We repeat, no impacts from Hurricane #Dorian will be felt across Alabama. The system will remain too far east."

From the Desk of Aldous J. Pennyfarthing
To: Donald Trump, Category 6 shitstorm

Dear Pr*sident Assclown,

Uh, people who live in Alabama and follow you on Twitter don't really need any help shitting their pants with fear. Instead of tweeting about a hurricane that has zero chance of hitting them, you could write literally any sentence with "Obama," "Second Amendment," and "transgender" in it and you'd fill every pair of pantaloons from Birmingham to Mobile with a 12-month doomsday bunker's ration full of creamy grits.

Also, the last time a president cared this much about what an actor was doing, he was getting shot in the back of the head at Ford's Theatre. Your holiday nut log of a brain most likely won't get that reference, of course. It has to do with Abraham Lincoln — one of the many, many presidents you think you've outshined during your brief reign of torpor.

Debra Messing? Really? *This* is what you're focused on? Hurricane Will & Grace?

Though Hurricane "Dorian" does make me wonder if there's a picture of you in a closet somewhere that's learning and maturing like a normal adult.

Yeah, you won't get that reference either. I might as well scrawl these bons mots on the back cover of a Bible and stick it in your vegetable crisper.

Finally, "I'm not sure that I've ever even heard of a Category 5."

Dude, we've had *four* Category 5 hurricanes *since you've been president.* Did one of them send a crack pipe through your head? I'm getting older, too, and my memory's not what it used to be, but Jesus Triscuit-Eatin' Christ, I've heard of a Category 5 hurricane before.

I mean, of the four Category 5 hurricanes we've had since 2017, you've really only ignored one of them. So there's no excuse for forgetting, man.

Here's a tip: Buy some ginkgo biloba; shove it up your ass because it's useless, and so are you; and cut your Adderall dose to 50 sinus-rattlin' Tony Montana snorts per day.

You'll feel much better. Believe me.

Love,
Pennyfarthing

September 2, 2019

- Trump tweets, "The LameStream Media has gone totally CRAZY! They write whatever they want, seldom have sources (even though they say they do), never do 'fact checking' anymore, and are only looking for the 'kill.' They take good news and make it bad. They are now beyond Fake, they are Corrupt."
- After canceling a trip to Poland to "monitor" Hurricane Dorian, Trump heads to his Virginia golf course for some leisure time.

September 3, 2019

- CNBC reports that Treasury Secretary Steven Mnuchin and U.S. Trade Representative Robert Lighthizer had to summon "multiple CEOs" to convince Trump not to double existing tariffs on China.
- Former Defense Secretary James Mattis says he may not stay silent about his days in the Trump administration forever, claiming "when the time's right to speak out about policy or strategy, I'll speak out."
- The Trump administration cancels $3.6 billion in military construction projects and diverts the money to Trump's vanity wall.

September 4, 2019

- Trump holds up a weather map that's been doctored with a Sharpie to "prove" Alabama had been in the path of Hurricane Dorian.

From the Desk of Aldous J. Pennyfarthing
To: Donald Trump, morning weathered man

Dear Pr*sident Assclown,

Jebus Giblets, I haven't seen this much controversy about the weather since NBC shoved Willard Scott out to sea on an ice floe.

What the fuck was that? Seriously.

If we could solve our problems that easily with a Sharpie, I would have replaced your head with a canned haggis ages ago.

I can only imagine the dick pics you're sending out to underage models. They must be at least 98 percent wet marker.

Here's a free humaning tip: It's okay to be wrong every once in a while. Everyone does it. It's how we grow. As long as we admit our mistakes, that is.

Something tells me our country is learning that lesson as we speak.

Love,
Pennyfarthing

September 5, 2019

- After the government reports the economy created 130,000 jobs in August, Trump tweets, "Really Good Jobs Numbers!" Here's what he tweeted on December 7, 2012, after the Bureau of Labor Statistics announced 146,000 jobs had been created under Obama (the number was later revised upward to 158,000): "Today's job report is not a good sign & we could be facing another recession. No real job growth. We need over 300K new jobs a month."

September 6, 2019

- Politico reports that the House Oversight Committee has been investigating why an Air Force crew stayed at Trump's Turnberry resort in Scotland and refueled at a nearby airport. A senior Air Force official told the site that the stay was "unusual" for the mission in question.
- The NOAA releases a statement that appears to back Trump in his ongoing feud with consensus reality. The NOAA also appears to throw the Birmingham NWS station, which correctly told Alabamans on September 1 that they were in no danger from Hurricane

- Dorian, under the bus: "The Birmingham National Weather Service's Sunday morning tweet spoke in absolute terms that were inconsistent with probabilities from the best forecast products available at the time."
- The NOAA's statement on Hurricane Dorian draws rebukes from several meteorological professionals, including former head of the National Hurricane Center Bill Read, who writes, "As I see it there are two possible drivers leading to the statement. Either NOAA Leadership truly agrees with what they posted or they were ordered to do it. If it is the former, the statement shows a lack of understanding of how to use probabilistic forecasts in conjunction with other forecast information. Embarrassing. If it is the latter, the statement shows a lack of courage on their part by not supporting the people in the field who are actually doing the work. Heartbreaking."

September 7, 2019

- Trump tweets, "Unbeknownst to almost everyone, the major Taliban leaders and, separately, the President of Afghanistan, were going to secretly meet with me at Camp David on Sunday. They were coming to the United States tonight. Unfortunately, in order to build false leverage, they admitted to an attack in Kabul that killed one of our great great soldiers, and 11 other people. I immediately cancelled the meeting and called off peace negotiations."

From the Desk of Aldous J. Pennyfarthing
To: Donald Trump, poo-resident of the U.S.

Dear Pr*sident Assclown,

So you were gonna invite the Taliban to Camp David to, what, commemorate the anniversary of 9/11? Uh ... maybe not the best optics?

Seriously, though. If Obama had tried to host the Taliban on U.S. soil during the anniversary of 9/11, Republicans would have shit enough bricks to rebuild the World Trade Center towers. But you do it and ... crickets.

So what *would* you have to do to outrage all those super-patriotic Republicans? Replace the 9/11 memorial with an 800-foot statue of bin Laden fisting Ronald Reagan? I bet that still wouldn't matter to them unless you made it out of melted guns you'd personally ripped out of their hands.

So here's a little drinking game I've invented: Every time Donald Trump screws something up beyond all reason, I swallow as much booze as I can until I pass out. If I survive the alcohol poisoning, the ER nurses have to drink.

To review, here's how you screwed up this one.

From *The New York Times*:

> When Mr. Khalilzad left Doha after the last round of talks concluded on Sept. 1, two days after the Situation Room meeting, he and his Taliban counterparts had finalized the text of the agreement, according to people involved. Leaders of both teams initialed their copies and handed them to their Qatari hosts.
>
> Before the end of the meeting, Mr. Khalilzad brought up the idea of a Taliban trip to Washington. Taliban leaders said they accepted the idea — as long as the visit came after the deal was announced.
>
> That would become a fundamental dividing point contributing to the collapse of the talks. Mr. Trump

did not want the Camp David meeting to be a celebration of the deal; after staying out of the details of what has been a delicate effort in a complicated region, Mr. Trump wanted to be the dealmaker who would put the final parts together himself, or at least be perceived to be.

So, yeah, another historic milestone to further distinguish your awesomely historic presidency — kind of like NASA's first-ever zero-gravity shart.

Enjoy the accolades.

Love,
Pennyfarthing

September 8, 2019

- After Trump attacks John Legend and his wife, Chrissy Teigen, on Twitter, Teigen tweets, "lol what a pussy ass bitch. tagged everyone but me. an honor, mister president."

◆ ◆ ◆

September 9, 2019

- After Hurricane Dorian hits the Bahamas, Trump says of refugees from the country, "I don't want to allow people that weren't supposed to be in the Bahamas to come into the United States — including some very bad people and very bad gang members."
- Trump tweets, "I know nothing about an Air Force plane landing at an airport (which I do not own and have nothing to do with) near Turnberry Resort (which I do own) in Scotland, and filling up with fuel,

- with the crew staying overnight at Turnberry (they have good taste!). NOTHING TO DO WITH ME."
- *The New York Times* reports that Commerce Secretary Wilbur Ross "threatened to fire top employees at the federal scientific agency responsible for weather forecasts … after the agency's Birmingham office contradicted President Trump's claim that Hurricane Dorian might hit Alabama."
- CNN reports that the U.S. successfully extracted a high-level covert asset from Russia in 2017 because of "concerns that President Donald Trump and his administration repeatedly mishandled classified intelligence and could contribute to exposing the covert source as a spy." The decision came after Trump spilled classified information to Russian Foreign Minister Sergey Lavrov and then-Russian Ambassador to the U.S. Sergey Kislyak during a May 2017 meeting in the Oval Office.

From the Desk of Aldous J. Pennyfarthing
To: Donald Trump, Putin's piss boy

Dear Pr*sident Assclown,

Wow, that's a red-letter day for our nation's first orange president.

Racism, open corruption, gaslighting/abuse of office, and rank incompetence/treason-ish behavior. That's *nearly* a full day for you. But I'm sure you can squeeze a few more outrages in. Have you tried eating a live bald eaglet with a dirty Taco Bell spork while wearing an original copy of the Constitution like a lobster bib?

What the fuck is wrong with you, you globose sack of disease-vectoring dildos?

Let's review the day's litany of dipshittery, shall we?

1) You're worried about "some very bad people and very bad gang members" fleeing the Bahamas for safety. It's just a wild coincidence that the country's population is 85 percent black, right?

2) In my experience, people who are totally innocent often write their denials in all caps. Because what kind of wanton, back-jungle, diarrheal-howler-monkey shit-midden would ever profane the sacred implicit promise inherent in ALL FUCKING CAPS, which assures us that every jot, tittle, and exuberant-dick-chafing pen stroke will be 1,001 percent true?

3) Wait, you threatened to ruin the careers and lives of the top people at the NOAA because you needed to be more right than they were about the *weather* — which happens to be their expertise? They don't come to your job and knock the bucket of chicken off *your* lap.

4) Oh, this one's my favorite. You spilled secrets to the Russians in the Oval Office so we had to extract one of our covert assets. So you're either an idiot, a traitor, or a tridiot. Well done, Brokedick Arnold.

Love,
Pennyfarthing

September 10, 2019

- Trump tweets that he's fired National Security Adviser John Bolton. Bolton insists that he resigned.

September 11, 2019

- On the 18th anniversary of the 9/11 attacks, Trump

tweets, "If it weren't for the never ending Fake News about me, and with all that I have done (more than any other President in the first 2 1/2 years!), I would be leading the 'Partners' of the LameStream Media by 20 points. Sorry, but true!"

- Explaining why his administration was cracking down on flavored e-cigarettes, Trump says, "We can't have our youth be so affected. And I'm hearing it — and that's how the first lady got involved. She's got a son, together, that is a beautiful young man. And she feels very, very strongly about it."

From the Desk of Aldous J. Pennyfarthing
To: Donald Trump, Grumplestilskin

Dear Pr*sident Assclown,

Did you just forget that Melania's son is also, uh, *your* son? Because that's totally what it looks like.

Just because Barron refers to you as "Mommy's anonymous sperm donor" doesn't mean you don't have some obligation to acknowledge him.

Granted, if you were *my* dad I'd probably start telling people I was Richard Speck's kid. Who's gonna check? Or I'd say I was grown in a lab from mushroom spores and orangutan shit. Or that I was a foundling. Or the result of a miraculous virgin birth. Or an alien sent here to kick ass and eat Corn Nuts, and I'm all out of Corn Nuts. Or a super-realistic hologram. Or a mass hallucination. Or an archangel who was kicked out of heaven because he wouldn't stop saying "literally." Or I'd just spend the rest of my life circling the Earth in a hot-air balloon while dressed as the Hamburglar so I'd never have to answer questions about my paternity.

Anything—anything—but acknowledging you were my father.

That scream Luke Skywalker let out when he found out Darth

Vader was his dad? Add a couple of zeroes and multiply it by π. That's what's in your kid's head 24/7. I'm surprised SETI's dishes haven't picked up his banshee-screeching brain waves by now.

So, yeah, you've probably done him a favor. Maybe just put him in the witness protection program. Give him a fresh start. If you were worth half a shit, you'd do that posthaste.

Love,
Pennyfarthing

September 12, 2019

- Trump claims that he looks orange because of energy-efficient light bulbs: "People said what's with the light bulb? I said here's the story, and I looked at it: The bulb that we're being forced to use — No. 1, to me, most importantly, the light's no good. I always look orange."
- During a speech in Baltimore, Trump refers to the vice president as "Mike Pounce."

From the Desk of Aldous J. Pennyfarthing
To: Donald Trump, Mister Shouty McNonsense

Dear Pr*sident Assclown,

So you can't remember the name of your own vice president and you think you look orange because of energy-efficient light bulbs.

I'm confused. When exactly did you shart your brains down your Zubaz? Because I'd have thought the media would have covered that. Maybe not as thoroughly as Hillary's dizzy spells, but still.

Here's a quick heads-up: You look orange because *you're fucking orange*, you congealed Muppet turd.

I use plenty of energy-efficient light bulbs. None of them have ever given me a creepy, otherworldly hue. I mean, you look like Picasso got blotto on absinthe and Keystone Light, shoved the handle end of a meat cleaver up his ass, carved 40 jack-o'-lanterns with it, and picked out the worst one.

Seriously, the only light you wouldn't look orange in is no light. And even then I can't guarantee you wouldn't spontaneously develop a self-illuminating phosphorescent orange glow just to be an asshole.

Also, Mike Pounce? What the fuck? How hard is it to remember "Pence"? I mean, you can be forgiven for not remembering Mike Pence the person. But the name? It couldn't get much easier than that. One syllable, no curveballs.

Sheesh. Get your fucking head checked for termites. I'm concerned. Truly.

Love,
Pennyfarthing

September 13, 2019

- *The Wall Street Journal* reports that, while awaiting a meeting with Egyptian President Abdel Fattah Al Sisi, Trump "looked over a gathering of American and Egyptian officials and called out in a loud voice: 'Where's my favorite dictator?'"

September 14, 2019

- For some reason, Trump quotes one of his most-mocked tweets of all time, writing, "'A Very Stable Genius!' Thank you."

September 15, 2019

- After *The New York Times* reports on a previously unknown sexual assault allegation against Brett Kavanaugh that the FBI never followed up on, Trump tweets, "Brett Kavanaugh should start suing people for liable [sic], or the Justice Department should come to his rescue. The lies being told about him are unbelievable. False Accusations without recrimination. When does it stop? They are trying to influence his opinions. Can't let that happen!"
- Despite having repeatedly said he'd meet with Iran without preconditions, Trump tweets, "The Fake News is saying that I am willing to meet with Iran, 'No Conditions.' That is an incorrect statement (as usual!)."
- Trump tweets, "Saudi Arabia oil supply was attacked. There is reason to believe that we know the culprit, are locked and loaded depending on verification, but are waiting to hear from the Kingdom as to who they believe was the cause of this attack, and under what terms we would proceed!"

From the Desk of Aldous J. Pennyfarthing
To: Donald Trump, war minger

Dear Pr*sident Assclown,

So, what? You're literally taking your orders from Prince Bone Saws now? So what if Saudi Arabia said they think the culprit was Jamal Khashoggi's grandfather and they think we should cut him into vertical slices and turn him into smoky jalapeño beef jerky? What then? You'd fucking do it, wouldn't you?

Also, you do realize where the 9/11 hijackers came from, right? We're just going to be at their beck and call now regardless of the circumstances?

What's your deal, anyway? You seem to have no problem whatsoever bowing and scraping in front of the world's worst dictators, but if you were ever forced to say anything nice about Angela Merkel your asshole would prolapse so fast it would set off car alarms in Georgetown.

Try to get this through your petrified head. The U.S. military is not a mercenary force. They work for *us*, not countries where you want to build towers. And they sure as shit don't give us orders. Well, they're not supposed to, anyway.

Love,
Pennyfarthing

September 16, 2019

- During a speech in New Mexico to *win over Hispanic voters*, Trump says, referring to CNN contributor Steve Cortes, "He happens to be Hispanic, but I never quite figured it out because he looks more like a WASP than I do." He then asks Cortes, "Who do you like more, the country or the Hispanics?"
- Trump claims that former Secretary of Defense James Mattis once told him that Obama had stuck Trump with a military that was "very low on ammunition."
- Mike Pence stays at a Trump hotel in Ireland that's 180 miles away from his meetings in Dublin.
- Asked about an Elizabeth Warren rally that drew 20,000 supporters, Trump says, "Certainly, if I went to Manhattan, if I went there — No. 1, she didn't have 20,000 people and No. 2, I think anybody would get a

good crowd there. I think you have a good crowd there if you don't even go there, just say you're going and how many people are in the park."

From the Desk of Aldous J. Pennyfarthing
To: Donald Trump, Whiny the Pooh

Dear Pr*sident Assclown,

Oh, Donny. You're such a sad little boy. You started a dick-measuring contest with a woman, and lost.

Then again, you *are* a noted expert on crowd sizes. The inauguration; crowd estimates that exceed arenas' capacity; that time you claimed thousands of people were watching your rally outside on a "tremendous movie screen" ... that didn't exist; the lines around the block to get into the Chuck E. Cheese birthday party room you booked for your campaign kickoff speech. It's all bullshit, man.

Most people at your stage of intellectual development have just one imaginary friend. Maybe two. You, apparently, have hundreds of thousands.

So I don't even know how to extrapolate a real number from your bullshit claims. For instance, you said you lost "hundreds" of friends during the 9/11 attacks, when the actual number was zero. If it had been *one* friend we could have easily derived the true number of ralleygoers with an equation that calculates proportions. But you can't *divide* by zero. Yes, that's right — even Fields Medal-winning mathematicians can't decipher your lies. Congrats.

By the way, *The Washington Post* did a fact-check on your numerous, shall we say, exaggerations about your crowd sizes. (Google "President Trump's crowd-size estimates: Increasingly unbelievable.")

You lie about this *all the time*. So I guess it only makes sense you think everyone does likewise.

Then there was this tweet, from August 27:

> "They do stories so big on Elizabeth 'Pocahontas' Warren's crowd sizes, adding many more people than are actually there, and yet my crowds, which are far bigger, get no coverage at all. Fake News!"

Oh, you precious little snowflake. Your life is so, so hard. Did you lose your binky again? It's not your turn to talk, so just shush. You'll get your chance. Here's a cinnamon graham cracker and a nice tall glass of shut the fuck up.

Love,
Pennyfarthing

September 17, 2019

- On the day of Cokie Roberts' death, Trump says of the veteran journalist, "I never met her. She never treated me nicely. But I would like to wish her family well. She was a professional and I respect professionals. ... Never treated me well, but I certainly respect her as a professional."

September 18, 2019

- Former Secretary of State Rex Tillerson says Israeli officials, including Prime Minister Benjamin Netanyahu, "played" Trump.
- Trump visits the U.S.-Mexico border to talk about his vanity wall. After discussing some of the wall's technological features, Lt. Gen. Todd Semonite, acting

head of the Army Corps, says, "Sir, there could be some merit in not discussing that."

From the Desk of Aldous J. Pennyfarthing
To: Donald Trump, hairy wallbanger

Dear Pr*sident Assclown,

"Sir, there could be some merit in not discussing that" is diplomatic military-speak for "Jesus Christ, you fucking shite-for-brains horse's ass. Shut that worthless simulacrum of an anus in the middle of your spray-tanned-manatee-undercarriage of a face."

So here's the dumbass quote Semonite was responding to:

"One thing we haven't mentioned is technology. They're wired so that we will know if somebody's trying to break through."

I don't even suffer from the febrile delusion that a sad row of metal posts with baby monitors duct-taped to them will somehow thwart the multibillion-dollar drug cartels, and yet *I* know better than to regurgitate this kind of information.

But, hey, you're proud of the (so far nonexistent) wall. It's your baby. Of course, so is Barron, and you never really talk about *him*.

Not that it matters what secrets you ultimately spill about this.

Here's how I see the cartels responding:

    1)   They eventually discover that your wall is equipped with advanced technology that detects when and where someone is trying to break through.
    2)   They continue to move their product through checkpoints and on ships and airplanes like they always have.
    3)   We waste billions of dollars on an ugly fence in the middle of the desert because your brain farts simply do not respond to Beano.

As for *people* sneaking over the border? Yeah, they'll figure out a way in. Wanna know how I know? BECAUSE THEY'RE PEOPLE AND NOT FUCKING ZOO ANIMALS.

But, whatever. Build the permanent monument to our nation's stupidity. Or we could just put a big bronze statue of you shitting in the National Mall reflecting pool and call it a day. Sure, it would be gross, but it would be a crucial reminder never to let this happen again and would ultimately save us $60 to $70 billion.

Love,
Pennyfarthing

◆ ◆ ◆

September 20, 2019

- Trump says the whistleblower who called Trump out over his conversation with Ukrainian President Volodymyr Zelensky is a "partisan." A minute later, he says he doesn't know who he or she is.
- Following an attack on Saudi Arabian oil facilities, Trump orders the deployment of additional U.S. troops to the country.

◆ ◆ ◆

September 21, 2019

- Trump tweets, "The Fake News Media and their partner, the Democrat Party, want to stay as far away as possible from the Joe Biden demand that the Ukrainian Government fire a prosecutor who was investigating his son, or they won't get a very large amount of U.S. money, so they fabricate a story about me and a perfectly fine and routine conversation I had with the

new President of the Ukraine. Nothing was said that was in any way wrong, but Biden's demand, on the other hand, was a complete and total disaster. The Fake News knows this but doesn't want to report!"
- Trump tweets, "The LameStream Media had a very bad week. They pushed numerous phony stories and got caught, especially The Failing New York Times, which has lost more money over the last 10 years than any paper in history, and The Amazon Washington Post. They are The Enemy of the People! The Fake News Media nowadays not only doesn't check for the accuracy of the facts, they knowingly make up the facts. They even make up sources in order to protect their partners, the Democrats. It is so wrong, but they don't even care anymore. They have gone totally CRAZY!!!!"

From the Desk of Aldous J. Pennyfarthing
To: Donald Trump, overlord projector

Dear Pr*sident Assclown,

Okay, nearly every single word in that tweet applies directly to you.

Let's review.

1) Had a very bad week => you
2) Lost more money [in] 10 years than anyone => also you
3) Enemy of the People => definitely you
4) Knowingly make up the facts => That describes you better than anything, like, ever.
5) "It is so wrong, but they don't even care anymore." => Whoa, this is fucking uncanny.
6) "They have gone totally CRAZY!!!!" => If you added a dozen or so unnecessary exclamation points, this would be you, too.

But you *are* a master projectionist, so I guess this is to be expected.

I look forward to the day when we have a president who's marginally more self-aware than a sea pineapple's sphincter.

Love,
Pennyfarthing

◆ ◆ ◆

September 23, 2019

- During a press conference with Polish President Andrzej Duda, Trump wails about the "double standard" involved in the brewing controversy over the Ukraine whistleblower complaint: "If a Republican ever did what Joe Biden did, if a Republican ever said what Joe Biden said, they'd be getting the electric chair by right now." He also takes another feckless swing at the media: "Look at the double standards. You people ought to be ashamed of yourself. And not all. We have some great journalists around. But you got a lot of crooked journalists. You're crooked as hell."
- *The Washington Post* reports that Trump ordered a hold on nearly $400 million in aid to Ukraine just days before calling its president and asking him to investigate Joe Biden's son, Hunter.
- Responding to teenage climate activist Greta Thunberg's impassioned speech to the UN, Trump sarcastically tweets, "She seems like a very happy young girl looking forward to a bright and wonderful future. So nice to see!"
- During a meeting with Pakistani Prime Minister Imran Khan, Trump says, "I think I'm going to get a Nobel Prize for a lot of things, if they gave it out fairly,

which they don't."

From the Desk of Aldous J. Pennyfarthing
To: Donald Trump, piss corpse

Dear Pr*sident Assclown,

Okay, I know I break your balls a lot, but let's give you the benefit of the doubt and take a serious look at your claim.

There are six Nobel Prize categories. Let's review, shall we?

- Physics
- Chemistry
- Medicine
- Literature
- Peace
- Economics

You think you'll get a Nobel for "a lot of things." Hmm. "A lot of things" is a pretty subjective measure, but I think most people would agree that has to be more than just two things.

So which ones do you think you should get?

Physics? In the late 16th century, Galileo proved that a tiny pebble and a morbidly obese orange man with fungal genitalia fall at the same rate in a vacuum. Acceleration due to gravity for both is roughly 32 feet/second^2. So there's not much you can tell us about that. But by all means, feel free to repeat the experiment.

Chemistry? Proving that repellent old men who look like Dr. Zaius swallowed 16 cubic meters of helium can be attracted to their own daughters is probably not what Alfred Nobel had in mind. So, no. Not that one either.

Medicine? They don't give out Nobels for people who subsist almost entirely on chicken skin and aspartame and manage to somehow live past 70. Maybe they should, but they don't. So you're not getting that one.

Literature? Please.

So that leaves Peace and Economics. As you can see, that's only two. Not "a lot."

Maybe, in a fairer world, conducting a natural experiment wherein you crash the global economy, thereby proving that trade wars are really fucking stupid and impossible to win, would net you a Nobel. But, as you pointed, this isn't a fair world. Sadly, it's biased against shit-slurping idiots. Not fair at all.

And Peace? This would actually be interesting, because I don't think they've ever given it out to anyone who encouraged his supporters to beat up protesters at political rallies, or who said he likes politicians who body-slam reporters. And it might be fun to hear a Nobel Peace Prize acceptance speech from a guy who sounds like an elderly hyena choking to death on an antelope's penis bone. I'm sure that's exactly the kind of thing the Nobel Committee is looking for. Because I know they're tired, and after you show up to claim your prize they can simply shut the door on modern civilization, turn off the lights, and enjoy the rhapsodic embrace of sweet, sweet death while basking in the glow of an Edenic paradise where the benighted conceits of Donald John Trump can no longer find purchase.

So, yeah, let's give you the Nobel Peace Prize. Sure. Whatever. But that's not "a lot of things." So you're still a fucking moron, Gilligan.

Love,
Pennyfarthing

◆ ◆ ◆

September 24, 2019

- Nancy Pelosi announces a formal impeachment inquiry into Trump over Trump's attempt to convince Ukrainian President Volodymyr Zelensky to investigate Joe Biden's son Hunter.

From the Desk of Aldous J. Pennyfarthing
To: Donald Trump, person of citrus

Dear Pr*sident Assclown,

Oopsies!

Someone get Nancy Pelosi a copy of *Forbes* with your face on it. Y'all's about to get *spanked!*

Love,
Pennyfarthing

◆ ◆ ◆

September 25, 2019

- Hours after releasing the transcript of Trump's call with Ukrainian President Volodymyr Zelensky, the White House accidentally sends its Ukraine-related talking points to Democratic lawmakers.
- Trump tweets, "There has been no President in the history of our Country who has been treated so badly as I have. The Democrats are frozen with hatred and fear. They get nothing done. This should never be allowed to happen to another President. Witch Hunt!"
- During a very low-energy press conference at the UN, Trump appears to rope Vice President Mike Pence into the growing Ukraine scandal, saying, "I think you should ask for VP Pence's conversation because he had a couple of conversations also."

From the Desk of Aldous J. Pennyfarthing

To: Donald Trump, arsenic and old face

Dear Pr*sident Assclown,

Yeah, nice speech, Eeyore. Are you feeling a bit Low-Energy Jeb?

Apparently, we need to put you in cryogenic freeze until science finds a cure for very, very low energy.

So today you came down from the prospectin' camp what's a spell up the mountain by the crick near the big rock next to Farmer Olsen's hunner'-year-old oak tree to ramble incoherently about this and that and the other.

And then in the middle of your dewy shart of a monologue you snuck in this little gem:

> "I think you should ask for VP Pence's conversation because he had a couple of conversations also. I could save you a lot of time; they were all perfect. Nothing was mentioned of any import other than congratulations. But the word is that they're going to ask for the first phone conversation. You can have it any time you need it, and also Mike Pence's conversations, which were, I think one or two of them. They were perfect. They were all perfect."

Whoa. Did you think we wouldn't catch that? The part where you subtly throw Mike Pence under the bus? Oh, yeah, you'll be goddamned if that creepy white-haired Children of the Corn motherfucker ever becomes president.

And who's next in line to the presidency after Pence? Well, Nancy Pelosi, of course.

Well played, Donny!

By the way, you couldn't see it, but the look on Mike Pompeo's face during this "speech" is precious. He looks like he wants to stuff you in a big flour sack with a saddlebag full of horseshoes and drown you in the nearest river.

Ah, but that didn't happen. It's just business as usual for Pompeo and his colleagues — pretend the president of the United States isn't three jars of urine away from being Howard Hughes and get on with your day.

Love,
Pennyfarthing

❖ ❖ ❖

September 26, 2019

- The whistleblower complaint involving Trump's attempts to pressure Ukrainian President Volodymyr Zelensky is released. It reads, in part, "In the course of my official duties, I have received information from multiple U.S. Government officials that the President of the United States is using the power of his office to solicit interference from a foreign country in the 2020 U.S. election. This interference includes, among other things, pressuring a foreign country to investigate one of the President's main domestic political rivals. The President's personal lawyer, Mr. Rudolph Giuliani, is a central figure in this effort. Attorney General Barr appears to be involved as well."
- *The Wall Street Journal* reports that Trump's controversial call with Ukraine's president was hidden away in a secret server that's "so secretive that even top White House national-security aides don't have regular access."
- Trump hints that the individual who gave the whistleblower information on Trump's call with the Ukrainian president should be executed as a spy: "I want to know who's the person, who's the person who gave the whistleblower the information? Because

that's close to a spy. You know what we used to do in the old days when we were smart? Right? The spies and treason, we used to handle it a little differently than we do now."
- Trump tweets, "THE GREATEST SCAM IN THE HISTORY OF AMERICAN POLITICS!"

From the Desk of Aldous J. Pennyfarthing
To: Donald Trump, pie-brains grifter

Dear Pr*sident Assclown,

> "THE GREATEST SCAM IN THE HISTORY OF AMERICAN POLITICS!"

Yes. Yes, you are.

Freudian slip or a rare spark of lucidity?

I suppose we'll never know.

Love,
Pennyfarthing

❖ ❖ ❖

September 27, 2019

- *The Washington Post* reports that Trump told Russian Foreign Minister Sergei Lavrov and Russian Ambassador Sergey Kislyak during their infamous 2017 Oval Office meeting that he wasn't concerned about Russian meddling in the 2016 election.
- Trump tweets, "To show you how dishonest the LameStream Media is, I used the word Liddle', not Liddle, in discribing [sic] Corrupt Congressman Liddle' Adam Schiff. Low ratings @CNN purposely took the hyphen out and said I spelled the word little wrong. A small but never ending situation with CNN!"

From the Desk of Aldous J. Pennyfarthing
To: Donald Trump, Li'l Grabb'ner

Dear Pr*sident Assclown,

The hyphen?

What fucking hyphen?

The actual president of the United States doesn't know the difference between a hyphen and an apostrophe. This is a real thing. Let's all reflect somberly on that, shall we?

Let's see, I learned about hyphens and apostrophes in … the third grade? Do we have to go back and teach you fractions, too? Should we write "L" and "R" on your shoes? Teach you how to pee while standing? How to pet rabbits without breaking their spines? Just how far back do we have to go with this remedial fucknuttery?

I mean, it's probably not your fault that your pregnant mother huffed all the black shoe polish your dad had set aside for his minstrel shows. But why do we *all* have to suffer because you had awful parents?

Also, when sending out a tweet designed to prove you really are a great speller — honest and for true — you should probably spell check it before you hit "publish." What the fuck does "discribing" mean?

Mein Gott im Himmel, you're a fucking dunce. Did the coke spoon you entombed in your sinuses during your Studio 54 days finally wriggle its way into your occipital lobe?

Love,
Pennyfarthing

September 29, 2019

- Trump tweets, "'If the Democrats are successful in removing the President from office (which they will never be), it will cause a Civil War like fracture in this Nation from which our Country will never heal.' Pastor Robert Jeffress, @FoxNews"
- Trump tweets, "Like every American, I deserve to meet my accuser, especially when this accuser, the so-called 'Whistleblower,' represented a perfect conversation with a foreign leader in a totally inaccurate and fraudulent way. Then Schiff made up what I actually said by lying to Congress. His lies were made in perhaps the most blatant and sinister manner ever seen in the great Chamber. He wrote down and read terrible things, then said it was from the mouth of the President of the United States. I want Schiff questioned at the highest level for Fraud & Treason."
- Trump retweets a parody Twitter account called Trump but About Sharks, which exists solely to make fun of his hatred of sharks.

From the Desk of Aldous J. Pennyfarthing
To: Donald Trump, aka Horatio Pornblower

Dear Pr*sident Assclown,

I don't really care that you got duped into retweeting a Twitter account that only exists to make fun of you. I'm just using your latest pratfall an excuse to resurrect my favorite passage in the history of Western literature. From Stormy Daniels' 2011 interview with *InTouch* magazine:

> "The strangest thing about that night — this was the best thing ever. You could see the television from the little dining room table and he was watching Shark Week and he was watching a special about the U.S.S.

something and it sank and it was like the worst shark attack in history. He is obsessed with sharks. Terrified of sharks. He was like, 'I donate to all these charities and I would never donate to any charity that helps sharks. I hope all the sharks die.' He was like riveted. He was like obsessed. It's so strange, I know."

Do me a favor. If for some reason I ever get caught in a frightfully banal conversation with you about your hatred of sharks, remind me not to try to shut you up by agreeing to have sex with you.

It's literally all I'll ever want from you — and it's just common courtesy when you think about it.

Love,
Pennyfarthing

◆ ◆ ◆

September 30, 2019

- Several media outlets report that Trump pressed Australia's prime minister to help look into the origins of Robert Mueller's Russia investigation.
- Trump says his administration is trying to find out the identity of the whistleblower who ratted him out over Ukraine.
- Trump shares a Breitbart impeachment poll asking, "Do you stand with President Trump?" The results: 97.83 percent, yes; 2.17 percent, no. Trump comments, "THANK YOU!"

From the Desk of Aldous J. Pennyfarthing
To: Donald Trump, unscientific troll

Dear Pr*sident Assclown,

Oh, and I thought you might actually be in some kind of trouble.

Guess not. Move along, y'all. Nothing to see here.

Honestly, this is like asking *High Times* readers whether they'd rather live in Colorado or Jeff Sessions' basement. You'll get the answer you want but, well, so fucking what? It's like sticking your head up your own ass instead of getting a colonoscopy. (And then screaming THANK YOU!)

You might want a second opinion is all I'm saying.

Meanwhile, in the real world — where Adderall-dusted candy apples don't grow on lollipop trees — you're underwater on the impeachment question.

Here's what FAKE NEWS!!!!!!!!!!! CNN says:

> About half, 47%, support impeaching the President and removing him from office, up from 41% who felt that way in a CNN poll in May. The current level matches the high point for impeaching Trump in previous CNN polling — 47% said they felt that way in September 2018.
>
> The share who favor impeachment and removal from office now narrowly outpaces the share who say they don't feel that way — a first in CNN polling — although the two figures are within the poll's margin of sampling error. Opposition stands at 45% in the new poll, down from 54% who said so in May and the lowest point in CNN polling on this topic.

But I'm sure the unscientific Breitbart poll with the thousands of self-selected respondents is far more accurate. Because … well, it just has to be. Right?

Still, public opinion doesn't matter much, does it? Your fate lies in the stars — and by "stars" I mean Adam Schiff and Nancy Pelosi.

Say, maybe you should consult the auguries or the Oracle of Delphi or the tea leaves or a pile of chicken entrails or Nancy Reagan's astrologist. Can't hurt, right?

Love,
Pennyfarthing

◆ ◆ ◆

October 1, 2019

- Trump tweets, "Congratulations to President Xi and the Chinese people on the 70th Anniversary of the People's Republic of China!"
- A report in *The New York Times* reveals that Trump "had often talked about fortifying a border wall with a water-filled trench, stocked with snakes or alligators, prompting aides to seek a cost estimate. He wanted the wall electrified, with spikes on top that could pierce human flesh. After publicly suggesting that soldiers shoot migrants if they threw rocks, the president backed off when his staff told him that was illegal. But later in a meeting, aides recalled, he suggested that they shoot migrants in the legs to slow them down."

From the Desk of Aldous J. Pennyfarthing
To: Donald Trump, wall-worshiping wankface

Dear Pr*sident Assclown,

At long last, the ragu has slid off your linguine.

Okay, Dr. Evil. Great plan. Snakes or alligators, huh? *With frickin' lasers beams attached to their heads*, I hope.

Now, when you said you wanted to kill hurricanes with nuclear weapons, I thought, "Oh, there it is. The dumbest thing a human being has ever said or ever will say. We have a winner. At long last, Caligula can rest in peace."

But, to your credit, you're not one to rest on your laurels. Willy Wanker's Fucknuts Factory never stops churning out new product.

And here's my very favorite part:

> "... prompting aides to seek a cost estimate."

Man, I've had unproductive days at work — days spent flirting with coworkers, playing endless games of Tetris, turning my exhaustive collection of free '90s AOL disks into impenetrable Viking shield walls to guard against the tedious depredations of nosy supervisors.

But this? Fuck. Me.

Some poor White House underling, who as we speak is likely moments away from greedily quaffing a witch's cauldron full of molten pig iron, *was ordered to seek a cost estimate for a 2,000-mile water-filled trench stocked with snakes and alligators!*

How

Is

This

Possible?

After that, your idea to shoot immigrants in the legs seemed, in a weird way, refreshing — in that it was merely evil and not preposterously and *cartoonishly* evil.

Why are you still here? They could put a blond wig on one of those wavy inflatable dudes you see in front of car washes and no one would know the fucking difference.

Just leave already.

Please. I'm begging.

Love,

Pennyfarthing

October 2, 2019

- Politico reports that House investigators are looking into a report that people are booking rooms at Trump hotels without staying in them. House Oversight Committee member Rep. Gerry Connolly says, "Now we're looking at near raw bribery."
- Secretary of State Mike Pompeo admits he listened in on Trump's July 25 call to Ukrainian President Volodymyr Zelensky.
- Trump tweets, "Now the press is trying to sell the fact that I wanted a Moot [sic] stuffed with alligators and snakes, with an electrified fence and sharp spikes on top, at our Southern Border. I may be tough on Border Security, but not that tough. The press has gone Crazy. Fake News!"
- During a crazy press gaggle in the Oval Office, Trump, while sitting next to Finland's president, says, "Nancy Pelosi and Shifty Schiff, who should resign in disgrace, and Jerry Nadler and all of them, it's a disgrace what's going on. They've been trying to impeach me from the day I got elected. I've been going through this for three years." He also says, "Look, I think a whistleblower should be protected if the whistleblower's legitimate."

October 3, 2019

- While speaking to reporters on the South Lawn of the White House, Trump urges China to investigate Joe

and Hunter Biden.
- *The Washington Post* reports that an IRS official filed a whistleblower complaint saying that a Treasury Department appointee tried to interfere with the annual audit of Trump's or Mike Pence's tax returns.

October 4, 2019

- Text messages obtained by Congress show that two ambassadors appointed by Trump explicitly linked a Ukrainian investigation into the 2016 U.S. election with an official White House visit for Ukraine's president. One text, from former U.S. special representative for Ukraine negotiations Kurt Volker, said, "Heard from White House – assuming President Z convinces trump he will investigate / 'get to the bottom of what happened' in 2016, we will nail down date for a visit to Washington."
- Trump tweets, "'I think it's outrages [sic] that a Whistleblower is a CIA Agent.' Ed Rollins @FoxNews"
- CNN reports that Trump has tapped Jared Kushner to spearhead his impeachment strategy efforts.

From the Desk of Aldous J. Pennyfarthing
To: Donald Trump, golden toilet god

Dear Pr*sident Assclown,

Wait, I haven't checked my Callow Dipshits of the 21st Century page-a-day calendar in a few weeks. I've been busy putting the finishing touches on a new dance I call "Fetal Position Inside a Pitch-Dark, Muculent Spider Hole Buried Fathoms Beneath the Dank, Fusty Loam of the Willamette Valley in Oregon."

So am I right in assuming Kushner has solved Middle East peace and the opioid crisis?

Way to go, Little Lord Fauntleroy! Have a biscuit and a dollop of marmalade!

But wait, for some reason I was under the impression that Kushner was … what's the word? … oh, yeah: "fuckingstupidasshit."

I mean, this is the guy who told you to fire James Comey. That's got to be the dumbest political advice in the history of the republic, with the possible exception of whatever he ends up telling you about avoiding impeachment.

Do you give him the benefit of the doubt because he's your son-in-law? Assuming Ivanka's batteries are at least half charged, at *best* he's her second-smartest sex toy.

Kushner is known for buying an albatross of a building at a hugely inflated price and cozying up to Prince Bone Saws, and that's about it.

Here's some free advice, because I love you, Donald, and I don't want to see you get hurt: Instead of tapping Kushner, go down to your local library, look for the guy in the third-floor stacks vigorously masturbating to photos of irregular watermelons, and (assuming it isn't Kushner, of course), put *him* in charge of your impeachment defense.

Because Kushner is not the answer. You could precisely reproduce his brain's electrical activity by sitting in the backyard whipping wet pasta at a bug zapper. Just because he's fucked your daughter and you still haven't doesn't mean he's a man of great accomplishments. It just means he's a dipshit silver spoon … like you.

Love,
Pennyfarthing

October 5, 2019

- Trump tweets, "I'm hearing that the Great People of Utah are considering their vote for their Pompous Senator, Mitt Romney, to be a big mistake. I agree! He is a fool who is playing right into the hands of the Do Nothing Democrats! #IMPEACHMITTROMNEY"

From the Desk of Aldous J. Pennyfarthing
To: Donald Trump, fanny pack full of moldy dicks

Dear Pr*sident Assclown,

> "I'm hearing that the Great People of Utah are considering their vote for their Pompous Senator, Mitt Romney, to be a big mistake."

First of all, you "hearing" something simply means the voices in your head are temporarily louder than the languorous crunching of Extra Crispy chicken skin. No one is saying that, and you're not citing any polling. You just don't like what Mitt Romney — who recently tweeted, "By all appearances, the President's brazen and unprecedented appeal to China and to Ukraine to investigate Joe Biden is wrong and appalling" — is saying.

Secondly, uh, you can't impeach a senator. But according to your unwavering "I'm rubber and you're glue" policy, you kind of have to call for the "impeachment" of Romney.

But here's how FAKE NEWS!!!!!!! CNN sums up your latest methane-triggered cranium cave-in:

> Trump's tweet immediately drew questions on Twitter from people curious as to whether a senator can be impeached. The short answer is: no.
>
> Senators and members of Congress can't be "impeached" but they can be "expelled," according to Ar-

ticle 1, Section 5, of the US Constitution.

The article states: "Each House [of Congress] may determine the Rules of its proceedings, punish its members for disorderly behavior, and, with the concurrence of two-thirds, expel a member."

According to Senate.gov, since 1789, the Senate has expelled only 15 members, most for supporting the Confederacy during the Civil War.
It's not clear what Trump thinks Romney could be "impeached" or, in this case, expelled for.

It's not clear? It's *very* clear. You don't like Romney because he backtalks your stupid ass. And in your wee, unctuous lizard brain, that's more than enough reason.

Love,
Pennyfarthing

October 6, 2019

- Mark Zaid, the lawyer for the whistleblower who came forward with information about Trump's July 25 call with Ukrainian president Volodymyr Zelensky, says he represents a second whistleblower with firsthand knowledge that corroborates the first whistleblower's report.
- In a stunning act of betrayal, Trump announces he will withdraw U.S. troops from northern Syria, giving Turkey the green light for its incursion against our Kurdish allies, who fought on our behalf against ISIS. The decision draws bipartisan condemnation.

From the Desk of Aldous J. Pennyfarthing
To: Donald Trump, coward of the country

Dear Pr*sident Assclown,

Let's see, 11,000 Kurds died fighting ISIS on our behalf, and after one phone call from one of your dictator buddies you just abandon them?

What did *you* sacrifice in the fight against ISIS? A 10 a.m. tee time?

I already thought it would be difficult for any of our allies ever to take us seriously again, considering we elected a bloviating smegma golem as president. Now I *know* we're fucked.

I once dreamed of visiting Westminster Abbey in London. I guess I'll have to settle for the Medieval Times in Orlando. Say, would it be a glaring anachronism if a royal falcon shits in my Pepsi?

I'll take my answer off the air.

Thanks.

Love,
Pennyfarthing

❖ ❖ ❖

October 7, 2019

- Trump tweets, "As I have stated strongly before, and just to reiterate, if Turkey does anything that I, in my great and unmatched wisdom, consider to be off limits, I will totally destroy and obliterate the Economy of Turkey (I've done before!). They must, with Europe and others, watch over the captured ISIS fighters and families. The U.S. has done far more than anyone could have ever expected, including the capture of 100% of the ISIS Caliphate. It is time now for others in the region, some of great wealth, to protect their own territory. THE USA IS GREAT!"

October 8, 2019

- The White House sends a letter to House Speaker Nancy Pelosi and other leading Democrats saying it will refuse to cooperate with the House's "illegitimate" impeachment inquiry.
- The State Department orders U.S. ambassador to the EU Gordon Sondland not to testify in the House's impeachment inquiry.
- A *Washington Post*-Schar School poll reveals that 58 percent of Americans support the House's impeachment inquiry.

October 9, 2019

- *The New York Times* reports that the U.S. shared intelligence with Turkey that may have helped the country target Kurdish forces, which were instrumental in our fight against ISIS.
- Two associates of Rudy Giuliani, Lev Parnas and Igor Fruman, are arrested at Washington Dulles Airport on campaign finance charges.
- In a desperate attempt to excuse his betrayal of the Kurds, Trump says, "And as somebody wrote in a very, very powerful article today, they didn't help us in the Second World War, they didn't help us with Normandy, as an example. They mentioned names of different battles. But they're there to help us with their land. And that's a different thing. In addition to that we have spent tremendous amounts of money on

helping the Kurds in terms of ammunition, in terms of weapons, in terms of money, in terms of pay."
- *Esquire* publishes an excerpt from the upcoming *All the President's Women: Donald Trump and the Making of a Predator*. The book alleges 43 new allegations of inappropriate behavior toward women on the part of Trump, including 26 incidents involving unwanted sexual contact.

From the Desk of Aldous J. Pennyfarthing
To: Donald Trump, her space invader

Dear Pr*sident Assclown,

> I moved on her like a bitch. But I couldn't get there. And she was married. Then all of a sudden I see her; she's now got the big phony tits and everything. She's totally changed her look.
>
> You know, I'm automatically attracted to beautiful — I just start kissing them. It's like a magnet. Just kiss. I don't even wait. And when you're a star, they let you do it. You can do anything.
>
> Grab 'em by the pussy. You can do anything.

Oh, wait. I'm sorry. I was writing an email to my grandma. Didn't realize I was typing in Word instead of Outlook.

But while I have you here — what the fuck, R. Jelly? *More* of this unbelievably gross shit?

So I have a confession. I was so disgusted with this new revelation about your (alleged) groping of *even more* women that I created a hyperrealistic Trump doll and brought it to a voodoo priestess, but she told me it was a terrible idea to stick pins in a full colostomy bag no matter how laudable my intentions were.

Also, what's this happy horseshit?

"And as somebody wrote in a very, very powerful article today, they didn't help us in the Second World War, they didn't help us with Normandy, as an example."

You know who else didn't help us in Normandy — or in any other battle, for that matter? *Anyone* in your family. Oh, but a Senate committee did once investigate your dad for profiteering off government contracts after the war. So there's that.

Love,
Pennyfarthing

October 10, 2019

- Trump tweets, "From the day I announced I was running for President, I have NEVER had a good @FoxNews Poll. Whoever their Pollster is, they suck."
- After attacking Minnesota Rep. Ilhan Omar, who is a black Muslim, at a rally in Minneapolis, Trump says, "As you know, for many years, leaders in Washington brought large numbers of refugees to your state from Somalia." The remark draws raucous boos from the overwhelmingly white crowd.

October 11, 2019

- Acting Homeland Security Secretary Kevin McAleenan resigns.
- Former U.S. ambassador to Ukraine Marie Yovanovitch testifies that Trump pressured the State Department to remove her from her position.
- ABC News reports that the business relationship be-

- tween Rudy Giuliani, Lev Parnas, and Igor Fruman is the subject of an ongoing criminal investigation.
- Trump orders 2,800 additional troops, as well as fighter jets and missile defense weapons, to Saudi Arabia.
- Trump suggests that he would have won New York and California had it not been for voter fraud: "They'll be calling me from Nebraska, they'll be calling me from Iowa, they'll be calling me from that beautiful midsection which was so beautiful bright red. You know, you had a little blue on the edges. And if there was honest voting, I really think I would have won that, too. But there's not, there's not. Whatever they tell you, there's not." Trump lost California by nearly 4.2 million votes.

From the Desk of Aldous J. Pennyfarthing
To: Donald Trump, lord of the lies

Dear Pr*sident Assclown,

Ah, the hits. Yes, if not for voter fraud, you'd win every state. You'd win every district. You'd get every vote. Because who could possibly vote against you, Dear Leader? That winning smile. The unmatched integrity. The baldfaced lies. The rape accusations. The feral sense of entitlement. The vertiginous incompetence and dishonesty.

It all *screams* "landslide."

By the way, that "little blue on the edges" represents millions upon millions of people. They vote. Iowa soybean fields don't vote. They rot into the earth because of your daft trade war.

And, okay, let's play this game. You lost California by almost 4.2 million votes. Hillary Clinton got 62 percent of the state's vote —nearly double your 32 percent share. That's a metric fuck-ton of fraud, dude. You'd pretty much have to breed those voters in gestation pits like Saruman's orcs to overcome all your "honest" votes. Where's the evidence of *any* of this, you gauche Tournament of Choads Parade?

Yeah, you've got nothin'. Thought so.

Love,
Pennyfarthing

October 12, 2019

- An AP story on Trump's fateful call to Volodymyr Zelensky reveals that Trump "occasionally" hands the phone to his daughter Ivanka on such calls so she can speak to famous world leaders.

October 13, 2019

- As Turkey escalates its military operation in northern Syria, Defense Secretary Mark Esper announces that approximately 1,000 U.S. troops will leave the region "as safely and quickly as possible," per Trump's instructions. The order ends most of the U.S. military presence in the area.

October 14, 2019

- Facing backlash from his own party, Trump imposes sanctions on Turkey over the country's invasion of northern Syria.
- *The Washington Post* reports that Trump has made 13,435 false or misleading claims during his 993 days

in office.

From the Desk of Aldous J. Pennyfarthing
To: Donald Trump, aka Peen-occhio

Dear Pr*sident Assclown,

Okay, let me grab my abacus. (That's an ancient calculating tool, you perv. Get your head out of the gutter.)

So you've made 13,435 false or misleading claims in 993 days. That's 13.5 lies a day.

Jebus Jebediah Christ. How? I barely *say* 13 things a day. And these are just the statements *The Washington Post* bothers to fact-check.

I mean, I suppose if *The Post* followed me around every day trying to catch me in a lie they'd find one occasionally. Like when my wife asks me where all the Skittles are and I say, "I have no idea" — which isn't *technically* a lie but nevertheless probably deserves at least two Pinocchios, because what I'm *really* saying is I have no idea if they're in my stomach or my duodenum.

But that's just rascally, rakish, impudent little me. I could tell 13 lies a day and very few people would care. But you're allegedly president. It *matters* if the president is honest. And you, well, almost never are.

But we knew that three years ago, and yet here we are, being ruled over by a poor man's Soapy Smith.

Love,
Pennyfarthing

October 15, 2019

- Rudy Giuliani says he will defy a House subpoena re-

- lated to the impeachment probe.
- Mike Pence says he will not cooperate with the House's "self-proclaimed" impeachment inquiry.
- Trump tweets, "Just out: MEDIAN HOUSEHOLD INCOME IS AT THE HIGHEST POINT EVER, EVER, EVER! How about saying it this way, IN THE HISTORY OF OUR COUNTRY! Also, MORE PEOPLE WORKING TODAY IN THE USA THAN AT ANY TIME IN HISTORY! Tough numbers for the Radical Left Democrats to beat! Impeach the Pres." Impeach the Pres.? Don't mind if we do.
- The Daily Beast reports that Trump is convinced departed national security adviser John Bolton is behind the Ukraine scandal leaks.

From the Desk of Aldous J. Pennyfarthing
To: Donald Trump, aka Blarney Rubble

Dear Pr*sident Assclown,

You know, you're probably right that John Bolton is behind all these leaks. I mean, Bolton is what you'd get if the demon from *Child's Play* had possessed Orville Redenbacher instead. That caramel corn-looking motherfucker is evil to the core, yo.

Still, I love this excerpt from The Daily Beast's story:

> In the course of casual conversations with advisers and friends, President Trump has privately raised suspicions that a spiteful John Bolton, his notoriously hawkish former national security adviser, could be one of the sources behind the flood of leaks against him, three people familiar with the comments said. At one point, one of those sources recalled, Trump guessed that Bolton was behind one of the anonymous accounts that listed the former national security adviser as one of the top officials most disturbed by the Ukraine-related efforts

of Trump and Rudy Giuliani, the president's personal attorney who remains at the center of activities that spurred the impeachment inquiry.

"[Trump] was clearly implying [it, saying] something to the effect of, 'Oh, gee, I wonder who the source on that could be,'" this source said, referring to the president's speculation. Bolton, for his part, told The Daily Beast last month that allegations that he was a leaker in Trump's midst are "flatly incorrect."

Bwah ha ha ha ha. *Of course* it's him. Why did you think that reptilian fuck would ever stay loyal to you? His only two emotions are smug self-satisfaction and raging war boner.

Oh, and The Daily Beast also reported he's working on a book. That's simply delicious.

Seriously, though, who *isn't* going to write a memoir about their time in the Trump White House? You won't be able to fit all those books on the little cart they'll be wheeling around in your cellblock in three years or so.

I assume Bolton has a *lot* of things to say. He's barking mad, of course—but the enemy of my enemy is, well, still a sociopathic lunatic. That said, he could help take you down. And that would be more schadenfreude than I could hold in my heart all at once. So please, just give me a breather, okay?

Love,
Pennyfarthing

October 16, 2019

- The House votes 354-60 to condemn Trump's decision to remove U.S. troops from northern Syria.
- In a meeting on Syria, Trump experiences what Nancy

Pelosi later describes as a "meltdown" and calls her a "third-grade politician." His tantrum reportedly started after Pelosi told Trump, "All roads with you lead to Putin."
- After Nancy Pelosi stated Trump had a meltdown during their meeting on Syria, Trump tweets that Pelosi had a "total meltdown."
- Russian troops take over recently abandoned U.S. bases in Syria. A military official with the anti-ISIS coalition tells Business Insider, "Humiliation doesn't begin to cover what the U.S. forces are feeling right now."
- ProPublica obtains documents showing "stark differences in how Donald Trump's businesses reported some expenses, profits and occupancy figures for two Manhattan buildings, giving a lender different figures than they provided to New York City tax authorities. The discrepancies made the buildings appear more profitable to the lender — and less profitable to the officials who set the buildings' property tax."
- CNN reports that Trump made 129 false claims in the previous week, the most since the network started counting them in July.
- After betraying the Kurds, Trump says "they're not angels" and claims they're "more of a terrorist threat in many ways than ISIS." He also says, "And the Kurds are much safer right now" and "there's a lot of sand they can play with."
- Fox Business' Trish Regan obtains a crazy-as-shit letter Trump sent to Turkish president Erdogan.

From the Desk of Aldous J. Pennyfarthing
To: Donald Trump, Turkey jiver

Dear Pr*sident Assclown,

Wait a bloody second — are you trying to steal my shtick? *I* write the crazy letters, dude.

What kind of mutant larval monstrosity is parkouring through your cerebellum right now?

In the unlikely event someone has pulled the oak branch from your head since you wrote it, here's your recent letter to Turkish President Recep Tayyip Erdogan:

> Dear Mr. President:
>
> Let's work out a good deal! You don't want to be responsible for slaughtering thousands of people, and I don't want to be responsible for destroying the Turkish economy — and I will. I've already given you a little sample with respect to Pastor Brunson.
>
> I have worked hard to solve some of your problems. Don't let the world down. You can make a great deal. General Mazloum is willing to negotiate with you, and he is willing to make concessions that they would never have made in the past. I am confidentially enclosing a copy of his letter to me, just received.
>
> History will look upon you favorably if you get this done the right and humane way. It will look upon you forever as the devil if good things don't happen. Don't be a tough guy. Don't be a fool!
>
> I will call you later.

"Don't be a tough guy"? You do realize Erdogan isn't from Queens, right?

You are to diplomacy what your mother was to not dropping babies headfirst on the kitchen linoleum — i.e., this is just one more thing that you totally and effervescently suck at.

Add it to the enormous pile.

Love,
Pennyfarthing

October 17, 2019

- Vice President Mike Pence and Turkish president Recep Tayyip Erdogan agree to a five-day ceasefire to allow the Kurds to withdraw from northeast Syria.
- Energy Secretary Rick Perry announces he will resign.
- U.S. Ambassador to the EU Gordon Sondland testifies that Trump ordered him to work with Rudy Giuliani on Ukraine.
- Acting Chief of Staff Mick Mulvaney announces that the 2020 G7 summit will be held at Trump's Doral golf resort.

October 18, 2019

- Jon Sopel, the BBC's North America editor, reports that Turkish president Recep Tayyip Erdogan was offended by the kookaburra letter Trump sent him. "When the time comes necessary steps will be taken," Erdogan reportedly said.

October 19, 2019

- Following intense backlash, Trump abandons his plan to host the G7 summit at his Doral golf resort, tweeting, "I thought I was doing something very good for our Country by using Trump National Doral, in Miami, for hosting the G-7 Leaders. It is big, grand, on hundreds of acres, next to MIAMI INTERNATIONAL AIRPORT, has tremendous ballrooms & meeting rooms, and each delegation would have its own 50 to 70 unit building. Would set up better than other alternatives. I announced that I would be willing to do it at NO PROFIT or, if legally permissible, at ZERO COST to the USA. But, as usual, the Hostile Media & their Democrat Partners went CRAZY!"

From the Desk of Aldous J. Pennyfarthing
To: Donald Trump, tin cup dictator

Dear Pr*sident Assclown,

Yeah, we could hold the G7 at your resort, but I hear they're still working out the bugs.

Seriously, dude. Why would you invite *anyone* to your garish, swamp-adjacent bedbug hatchery, much less the world's most important leaders? It's humid, ungodly hot (especially in June, when the G7 is scheduled), and the place is permanently redolent of molted Trump rind.

Also, this, from The Daily Beast:

> One infestation in the main kitchen of Trump's Doral golf club in 2015 was so bad that health inspectors recommended that the place be temporarily shut down.

And this, from a July 2019 story in Quartz:

> Quartz revealed in May that the pools at Trump resorts in Florida have been cited for poor water quality and other health and safety violations far more frequently than other resorts. Florida Department of Health inspectors actually shut down pools at

Trump properties at least 10 times in the last year, state records show, while other luxury properties had mostly pristine pools.

So, sure, staying at Doral would be a *great* idea, unless you haven't had a tetanus shot in a few years.

But then this has nothing to do with the fact that Doral's revenue has been sagging like your Pleistocene scrotum in an equatorial rainforest — does it?

Sorry your grift didn't work this time. You can hatch a new scheme tomorrow. I'm sure it'll be a *yuuuuge* success.

Love,
Pennyfarthing

October 20, 2019

- Trump refers to Defense Secretary Mark Esper as "Mark Esperanto" on Twitter.

October 21, 2019

- Trump calls the Constitution's emoluments clause "phony."
- During an interview with Sean Hannity, Trump says, "They could've impeached Obama for the IRS scandal. They could impeach him for the guns for whatever where guns went all over the place and people got killed, Fast and Furious. They could've killed him — they could've impeached him for many different things."

From the Desk of Aldous J. Pennyfarthing

To: Donald Trump, genius envier

Dear Pr*sident Assclown,

My lord. Somewhere in the blessed, faraway ether Sigmund Freud just busted his spectral left nut from laughing too hard.

Yes, this was a … slip, of the Freudian variety. But, man, what a slip! And it arrives so soon after a Scottish fen full of "Obama could have been impeached" garble.

> "They could've impeached Obama for the IRS scandal. They could impeach him for the guns for whatever where guns went all over the place and people got killed, Fast and Furious. They could've killed him — they could've impeached him for many different things."

That's not a word salad. That's more like a word hog trough full of circus peanuts and premasticated gum.

We get it. You hate Barack Obama. I mean, he had the temerity to get elected president — twice! — while openly black. How dare he? But try to keep a lid on your rancid fantasies, okay?

Most of us love Barack Obama and still think of him as our president. To a great many of us, you replacing him felt like Mom divorcing Dad so she could date Carrot Top.

In other words, it's a fucking nightmare.

Try not to make it worse every single fucking day of your worthless life.

Love,
Pennyfarthing

October 22, 2019

- Bill Taylor, the U.S.' top diplomat in Ukraine, testifies that "everything" Ukraine wanted — including military aid and a White House meeting — depended on Ukraine's opening an investigation into Joe and Hunter Biden.
- Mitch McConnell flatly contradicts Trump's claim that McConnell told Trump his call to Volodymyr Zelensky was "the most innocent phone call that I've ever read." "I don't recall any conversations with the president about that phone call," McConnell says.
- Trump tweets, "So some day, if a Democrat becomes President and the Republicans win the House, even by a tiny margin, they can impeach the President, without due process or fairness or any legal rights. All Republicans must remember what they are witnessing here - a lynching. But we will WIN!"

From the Desk of Aldous J. Pennyfarthing
To: Donald Trump, racist douche

Dear Pr*sident Assclown,

I really need to upgrade to the Microsoft Office Suite with the 26-letter font made entirely of vomit emojis. Because the standard Latin alphabet just isn't doing the job anymore.

"A lynching."

Wow.

And *fuuuuuuuuuuuuuuuuuuuuuuucccccccccccccckkkkkkkkkk yoooooouuuuuuuuuu.*

I know your knowledge of U.S. history only goes back to the second season of *American Gladiators*, but that's no excuse.

In short, your being impeached in strict accordance with the rules set forth by the Constitution of the United States of America is in no way, shape, or form a "lynching." A lynching is what you tried to do to the Central Park Five.

I know you've set the bar for human decency lower than Rupert Murdoch's scrote, but this is the kind of comment that would have ended the career of a politician prior to 2015.

But, alas, we live in the upside-down now, so we're gonna need a much bigger scandal than this to get Republicans to turn against you. Like, say ... uh ... you know, I can't even imagine what that could be. Exhuming Ronald Reagan's body, making a headdress out of his bones, and declaring yourself emperor-for-life of Oceania?

Maybe that would do it?

Okay, probably not.

Love,
Pennyfarthing

October 23, 2019

- Trump announces that he's lifting sanctions on Turkey and that only a "small number" of U.S. troops will stay in Syria to guard the country's oil fields. During his speech announcing the move, Trump says, "Let someone else fight over this long-bloodstained sand."
- Trump's lawyers argue that Trump can't be prosecuted while in office even if he shoots someone in broad daylight on Fifth Avenue.
- During a speech in Pittsburgh, Trump says, "And we're building a wall on the border of New Mexico and we're building a wall in Colorado, we're building a beautiful wall, a big one that really works that you can't get over, you can't get under and we're building a wall in Texas." Colorado is not on the U.S.-Mexico border.

October 24, 2019

- *The Wall Street Journal* reports that the White House plans to order all federal agencies not to renew their subscriptions to *The Washington Post* and *The New York Times*.

From the Desk of Aldous J. Pennyfarthing
To: Donald Trump, William Randolph Fuckface

Dear Pr*sident Assclown,

Now how is the White House going to get all the news it needs from just Fox News and *Juggs*? And, frankly, how will anyone tell the difference?

So *The New York Times* and *Washington Post* are the most important newspapers in the country. There's really no question about that. You don't like them because they report factually about you.

This is some noisome wannabe dictator shit, dude.

Here's what retired four-star Gen. Barry McCaffrey tweeted about your move:

> "The White House Trump statement telling the entire Federal Government to terminate subscriptions to the NYT and Wash Post is a watershed moment in national history. No room for HUMOROUS media coverage. This is deadly serious. This is Mussolini."

Now, I've had my disagreements with McCaffrey. Mainly because he's a former government drug czar and my blood has more THC in it than Snoop Dogg's charter jet to Montego Bay. But he's 100 percent correct here.

You're basically Goebbels with poofier hair.

This is a *democracy*. Democracy dies in darkness, if it's not smothered by a large orange man's ass flaps first.

Love,
Pennyfarthing

October 25, 2019

- Trump tweets, "Another big dropout of the Presidential race was, along with 0% Tim Ryan, 0% @RepSwalwell. Such talk and bravado from both, and nothing to show. They stood for nothing, and the voters couldn't stand by them. Obnoxious and greedy politicians never make it in the end!"

October 26, 2019

- *The Washington Post* reports that Trump agreed to leave a small contingent of troops in Syria only after he was warned that pulling out entirely could cede control of the country's oil fields to someone else: "This is like feeding a baby its medicine in yogurt or applesauce," one official told the newspaper.
- *The Wall Street Journal* reports that U.S. Ambassador to the EU Gordon Sondland told House investigators that the pressure Trump exerted on Ukraine's government amounted to a quid pro quo: "Asked by a lawmaker whether that arrangement was a quid pro quo, Mr. Sondland cautioned that he wasn't a lawyer but said he believed the answer was yes."

October 27, 2019

- In a bizarre, macabre speech, Trump announces the death of ISIS leader Abu Bakr al-Baghdadi. At one point, Trump says of Baghdadi, "He died after running into a dead-end tunnel, whimpering and crying and screaming all the way."
- Trump attends game 5 of the World Series at Nationals Park in Washington, D.C., and is greeted with raucous boos and chants of "lock him up!"

From the Desk of Aldous J. Pennyfarthing
To: Donald Trump, Mr. Boo-urns

Dear Pr*sident Assclown,

Ooh. Ouchies.

That was … uh … kinda harsh.

You okay?

How are you gonna spin this one? Maybe you can say they were actually chanting "Burisma" because they really want Ukraine to investigate the Bidens. Yeah, that might work.

I can't even imagine what it's like to be booed by 41,000 people. And so vociferously. Wow. Just be glad it was Free Cap Night and not, say, Gallon Milk Jug Full of Beluga Whale Semen Night. You would have walked out of there looking like a giant Krispy Kreme doughnut.

Maybe just keep your fluorescent orange shit-falafel of a head draped in fancy veils whenever you're north of the Carolinas. You can tell yourself all you want that the polls are fake, but most people fucking *loathe* you, dude. Not just your wife.

Buck up, man. Eventually this will all be over. Then we can all forget about you and go back to loving Barack Obama.

Oh, Barack Obama. The very sound of his name is like sweet songs of seraphim to my weary, discontented ear holes.

Barack Obama, we praise you! We love you forever! Come back to us, oh infinite divine spirit!

Ah, I'm just breaking your balls. Obama's not a god or anything. Just a much, much, much, much, *much* better man than you.

Love,
Pennyfarthing

October 28, 2019

- At a speech before the International Association of Chiefs of Police, Trump appears to advocate committing war crimes in Syria: "But we're keeping the oil — remember that. I've always said that: 'Keep the oil.' We want to keep the oil. Forty-five million dollars a month? Keep the oil. We've secured the oil."
- Asked about Trump's claim that ISIS leader Abu Bakr al-Baghdadi was "whimpering and crying" before dying in a U.S.-led raid, Gen. Mark Milley, chairman of the Joint Chiefs of Staff, appears to contradict the pr*sident, saying, "I don't know what the source of that was."

October 29, 2019

- Lt. Col. Alexander Vindman testifies before a House committee looking into Trump's July 25 call with

Ukrainian President Volodymyr Zelensky. During his opening remarks, Vindman states, "I was concerned by the call. I did not think it was proper to demand that a foreign government investigate a U.S. citizen, and I was worried about the implications for the U.S. government's support of Ukraine. I realized that if Ukraine pursued an investigation into the Bidens and Burisma, it would likely be interpreted as a partisan play which would undoubtedly result in Ukraine losing the bipartisan support it has thus far maintained. This would all undermine U.S. national security."

- Trump tweets, "Why are people that I never even heard of testifying about the call. Just READ THE CALL TRANSCRIPT AND THE IMPEACHMENT HOAX IS OVER! Ukrain [sic] said NO PRESSURE."

From the Desk of Aldous J. Pennyfarthing
To: Donald Trump, reading lame beau

Dear Pr*sident Assclown,

Okay, the fact that you keep telling people to READ THE TRANSCRIPT suggests to me that you haven't actually, uh, read the transcript. Because it's really, really, *really* fucking incriminating, dude. Telling people to read it is like John Wayne Gacy inviting his neighbors into his crawl space for a few late-night games of foosball.

Also, it's NOT A TRANSCRIPT. How do I know? Because the "transcript" literally *says* it's not a transcript.

It's right there in the "transcript" you released, which is posted on whitehouse.gov for any fool to read:

> CAUTION: A Memorandum of a Telephone Conversation (TELCON) is not a verbatim transcript of a discussion. The text in this document records the notes and recollections of Situation Room Duty Officers

and NSC policy staff assigned to listen and memorialize the conversation in written form as the conversation takes place.

So there's that.

Also, the "transcript" is full of ellipses, which mark areas where the text has been bowdlerized.

FYI, "bowdlerized" means "expurgated."

FYI, "expurgated" means "removed."

FYI, "remove" is what Nancy Pelosi is going to do with your balls.

But I *do* have to give you credit for one thing. You're telling *your* followers to "read the transcript." Ha ha ha ha ha ha ha! That's a failsafe if I've ever seen one. You could have placed portions of the transcript on three separate encrypted servers and launched one to Andromeda, sunk the second into the Marianas Trench, and buried the third deep within the folds of your eternally avalanching moobs and they wouldn't have been any better hidden from your cult than this.

"Read the transcript." Hoo-boy, that's a good one.

Credit where it's due. Well done, Jigglenuts.

Love,
Pennyfarthing

October 30, 2019

- *The Washington Post* reports that White House lawyer John Eisenberg moved a transcript of Trump's July 25 call with Ukrainian President Volodymyr Zelensky to a highly classified server.

- Just before the new quarterly GDP number is released, Trump tweets, "The Greatest Economy in American History!" The report reveals that the GDP grew at an unspectacular 1.9 percent in Q3. And here's what he tweeted in May 2012 while Barack Obama was president: "Q1 GDP has just been revised down to 1.9% … The economy is in deep trouble."

October 31, 2019

- The House votes 232-196 to formalize the procedures of the Trump impeachment inquiry.
- Tim Morrison, the National Security Council's top Russia and Europe adviser, corroborates U.S. diplomat Bill Taylor's October 22 House testimony: "I reviewed the statement Ambassador Taylor provided this inquiry on October 22, 2019. I can confirm that the substance of his statement, as it relates to conversations he and I had, is accurate."
- Trump announces that he's switching his official place of residence from New York to Florida.
- Several media outlets report that Rudy Giuliani locked himself out of his iPhone in 2017, less than a month after Trump had named him his cybersecurity adviser. A former employee at the Apple store where Giuliani sought help called Giuliani's actions "very sloppy," telling NBC News: "Trump had just named him as an informal adviser on cybersecurity and here, he couldn't even master the fundamentals of securing your own device."

From the Desk of Aldous J. Pennyfarthing
To: Donald Trump, Julius Geezer

Dear Pr*sident Assclown,

Cybersecurity adviser, huh? Well, he kept himself out of his own phone; he sure did a bang-up job of that. Not sure if that means he can keep Russia from hacking our election again.

Seriously, though, making Rudy Giuliani your cybersecurity adviser is like appointing Mayor McCheese surgeon general. Actually, it's way worse. Mayor McCheese has some vague idea that vegetables are good for you. Rudy probably thinks cybersecurity is about keeping evil robots from the future from stealing his old-man erection diary.

Still, this is the least surprising news, like, ever. If you'd told me Rudy had locked himself in his own car in the Waffle House parking lot overnight I'd have had basically the same reaction. The guy's not all there, in case you hadn't noticed. Seriously, you'd get better legal advice from a Furby.

Love,
Pennyfarthing

November 1, 2019

- Responding to the latest government jobs report, Trump tweets, "Wow, a blowout JOBS number just out, adjusted for revisions and the General Motors strike, 303,000. This is far greater than expectations. USA ROCKS!" The actual number of jobs crated in October was 128,000.
- During a rally in Tupelo, Mississippi, Trump coins the words "foistered, delegitimitized, and apprenti."
- Trump tweets, "You can't Impeach someone who hasn't done anything wrong!"

From the Desk of Aldous J. Pennyfarthing
To: Donald Trump, my sweet impeachable you

Dear Pr*sident Assclown,

"You can't Impeach someone who hasn't done anything wrong!"

You're right.

Aaaaaaannnnddd ... they won't.

Good luck with your impeachment, Puddles. Should be a great time.

I'll bring the Jiffy Pop.

Love,
Pennyfarthing

November 2, 2019

- Trump attends a UFC match at New York's Madison Square Garden and is loudly booed for the second time in less than a week.
- *The Washington Post* reports that "[s]muggling gangs in Mexico have repeatedly sawed through new sections of President Trump's border wall in recent months by using commercially available power tools, opening gaps large enough for people and drug loads to pass through."

From the Desk of Aldous J. Pennyfarthing
To: Donald Trump, gorged wall-ass

Dear Pr*sident Assclown,

Hmm, who could have ever predicted that 21st century humans would figure out how to get past — or in this case, through — a wall?

I swear to God, you are dumber than your own colon polyps. All this money, all this rancor, a dangerous and costly government shutdown, and for what? A wall that can be sliced through "in minutes" with a saw that retails for $100 at Home Depot. That's like spending tens of billions developing a new Abrams M1 battle tank that can be taken down with the San Diego Chicken's T-shirt cannon.

So, sure, let's build 2,000 miles of your Great Wall of Fine China.

Oh, also, about three weeks ago this happened. An experienced rock climber built a replica of your wall and …

> Several people have already managed to climb up the wall replica, including 8-year-old Lucy Hancock. Hancock didn't use any ropes or other tools to climb the wall, but wore a belay, a safety device designed to catch a falling climber. An adult climber, Erik Kloeker, was up and over the wall in about 40 seconds. — *Time* magazine

An 8-year-old girl beat your "impenetrable" wall. *Eight fucking years old*, dude. So it's super easy to go over, through, under, or around your wall. (Does that cover everything? Any nearby wormholes or hot tub time machines you might have overlooked?) It's literally child's play. You might as well put up a velvet rope with a bouncer stationed every 3 miles. The William J. Le Petomane Thruway's tollbooth was harder to get around, for fuck's sake.

(Idea for future Democratic debates: The candidate who can get over your wall the fastest gets to speak first.)

So whaddaya say, Jimmy Green Grapes? When Mexicans are done hauling away your wall and selling it for scrap, will we have to pay them to get it back? That kind of sounds like the *opposite* of what you promised.

Love,
Pennyfarthing

November 3, 2019

- Trump tweets, "Virginia has the best Unemployment and Economic numbers in the history of the State. If the Democrats get in, those numbers will go rapidly in the other direction. On Tuesday, Vote Republican!" Virginia's governor, Ralph Northam, is a Democrat.
- Trump tweets, "If Shifty Adam Schiff, who is a corrupt politician who fraudulently made up what I said on the 'call,' is allowed to release transcripts of the Never Trumpers & others that are & were interviewed, he will change the words that were said to suit the Dems purposes. Republicans should give their own transcripts of the interviews to contrast with Schiff's manipulated propaganda."

November 4, 2019

- Columnist E. Jean Carroll, who in June accused Trump of raping her in a department store in the '90s, files a defamation suit against him for accusing her of lying about the encounter.
- The Second Circuit Court of Appeals rules that Trump can't block a subpoena forcing his accounting firm to hand over his tax returns to the Manhattan district attorney's office.
- In another sign that Trump's Iran policy is an abject failure, the chief of the country's nuclear program says they're operating twice as many advanced centrifuges as were previously reported.
- Trump tweets, "My son, @DonaldJTrumpJr is coming

out with a new book, 'Triggered: How the Left Thrives on Hate and Wants to Silence Us' – available tomorrow, November 5th! A great new book that I highly recommend for ALL to read. Go order it today!" The tweet appears to violate ethics rules prohibiting the use of one's office for private gain or for the benefit of family or friends.

From the Desk of Aldous J. Pennyfarthing
To: Donald Trump, the little dumberboy

Dear Pr*sident Assclown,

So will whoever wrote your son's book for him come out in 30 years to tell everyone what an effluvious turdnugget he is, like your ghostwriter did with you?

Incidentally, I would bet six pints of my own blood, deliverable upon request, that you haven't actually read this book. The other six I'd like to hold in reserve for the colossal boner I'll be coaxing like a cobra from my Batman and Robin Underoos when Ivanka shows up for her arraignment in her orange jumpsuit. Because your entire family is crooked as fuck, in case you hadn't noticed.

To wit:

> **§ 2635.702 Use of public office for private gain.**
> An employee shall not use his public office for his own private gain, for the endorsement of any product, service or enterprise, or for the private gain of friends, relatives, or persons with whom the employee is affiliated in a nongovernmental capacity, including nonprofit organizations of which the employee is an officer or member, and persons with whom the employee has or seeks employment or business relations.

But go ahead. Keep talking about how Joe Biden supposedly used his office to benefit his son.

By the way, the title of Don Jr.'s book is boring as fuck.

I'd suggest he go back to the drawing board and try out some of these:

- *Fredo!*
- *Trigger: My Life as a Horse's Ass*
- *Please, Dad, Don't Fuck My Girlfriend!*
- *I Grew a Beard! Look at It! Look! It's Magnificent!*
- *Triggered: How My Man-Baby Father Feels Every Morning After Googling His Name*
- *I Wrote a Book That No One Who Can Actually Read Would Ever Be Caught Dead Buying: The Donald Trump Jr. Story*
- *When I Turned 1, Dad Threw a Birthday Party for My Placenta, and Other Stories*
- *How to Live Your Life With Every Imaginable Privilege Without Ever Once Noticing*
- *Hey, At Least I'm Not Eric*
- *Daddy, Look at Me! Look at ME! For God's Sake, Love Me! Please!*

Tell Donny Spooge Stain he can have any of these titles for free.

Thanks, man.

Love,
Pennyfarthing

November 5, 2019

- Newly revealed phone records show that Trump called former *Apprentice* contestant Summer Zervos, who is suing Trump for defamation, around the same time he allegedly sexually assaulted her.
- U.S. Ambassador to the EU Gordon Sondland reverses

his testimony on Ukraine. According to Politico, "In his revised statement, Sondland said he now remembers telling a top Ukrainian official on Sept. 1 that hundreds of millions of dollars in military aid to the beleaguered U.S. ally would 'likely' be held up unless the government announced investigations of Trump's political rivals."

November 6, 2019

- The House releases the transcript of William Taylor's testimony. According to CNN, Taylor "told House impeachment investigators that President Donald Trump's personal attorney Rudy Giuliani was pressing Ukraine 'to intervene in US domestic policy or politics.'"
- *The Washington Post* reports that Trump wanted Attorney General Bill Barr to hold a press conference declaring that Trump had broken no laws in connection with his July 25 call with Ukrainian President Zelensky.
- After Republican Gov. Matt Bevin is defeated in the ruby red state of Kentucky, Trump tweets, "Our big Kentucky Rally on Monday night had a massive impact on all of the races. The increase in Governors race was at least 15 points, and maybe 20! Will be in Louisiana for @EddieRispone on Wednesday night. Big Rally!" He also tweets, "Based on the Kentucky results, Mitch McConnell @senatemajldr will win BIG in Kentucky next year!"

From the Desk of Aldous J. Pennyfarthing
To: Donald Trump, tea-bragger

Dear Pr*sident Assclown,

Uh huh. Kentucky is redder than your ass, pal. Losing the governorship is not exactly a triumph.

So if you're just gonna pull numbers out of your Donald Trump (a new synonym for "diseased asshole" I've been workshopping; whaddya think?), why limit it to 15 or 20 points? Why not say Bevin would have lost 20 million to 2 without your help? Your followers will evidently believe anything.

As for your prediction that Mitch McConnell will win BIG next year? Uh huh. We'll see. Because if there's anything redder than Kentucky, it's Moscow Mitch.

Love,
Pennyfarthing

◆ ◆ ◆

November 7, 2019

- As part of a settlement with the New York state attorney general's office, Trump is fined $2 million for misusing his nonprofit foundation for personal gain. The violations included using the charity to further his presidential campaign.
- *The Washington Post* publishes excerpts from the upcoming book *A Warning* by an anonymous White House official. Among the more eye-opening passages is this description of Trump's presidency: "It's like showing up at the nursing home at daybreak to find your elderly uncle running pantsless across the courtyard and cursing loudly about the cafeteria food, as worried attendants tried to catch him. You're stunned, amused, and embarrassed all at the same time. Only your uncle probably wouldn't do it *every single day*, his words aren't broadcast to the public, and he doesn't have to lead the US government once

he puts his pants on."

November 10, 2019

- Journalist Roger Sollenberger writes a piece for Salon in which he reveals that Rudy Giuliani, Donald Trump's informal cybersecurity expert, accidentally sent Sollenberger his computer/phone password.
- Trump tweets, "The call to the Ukrainian President was PERFECT. Read the Transcript! There was NOTHING said that was in any way wrong. Republicans, don't be led into the fools trap of saying it was not perfect, but is not impeachable. No, it is much stronger than that. NOTHING WAS DONE WRONG!"

From the Desk of Aldous J. Pennyfarthing
To: Donald Trump, perfect asshole

Dear Pr*sident Assclown,

PERFECT CALL! PERFECT CALL!

THAT CALL WAS PERFECT!

Who ate the strawberries?!?!?!

PERFECT, I TELLS YA!

Sheesh, man.

You seem to have an oddly specific form of Tourette's. Maybe get that checked. Or stop snorting your Adderall off the backs of psychedelic toads.

I suppose it's important to project confidence when your bowels are spilling out on the abattoir floor, but this behavior really makes me wonder what transcript you're reading. And on what planet.

Your call was basically a mob shakedown. The only person who would say it's perfect is John Gotti's lawyer. Everyone else sees a criminal doing egregious criminal shit.

Get some sleep. We'd all benefit.

Hey, wouldn't it be weird if you actually did sleep for, say, 12 hours and woke up perfectly normal? Then started reading the shit you've been doing for the past three years and immediately called a press conference to apologize for behaving like a mad raving dingo with a flaming wad of toilet paper up its ass?

One can dream, anyway.

Love,
Pennyfarthing

◆ ◆ ◆

November 11, 2019

- Trump appears to ask Republicans to release fake transcripts from the impeachment hearings, tweeting, "Shifty Adam Schiff will only release doctored transcripts. We haven't even seen the documents and are restricted from (get this) having a lawyer. Republicans should put out their own transcripts! Schiff must testify as to why he MADE UP a statement from me, and read it to all!"
- Trump tweets, "Vote for Sean Spicer on Dancing with the Stars. He is a great and very loyal guy who is working very hard. He is in the quarterfinals - all the way with Sean! #MAGA #KAG." Later that night, after Spicer is voted off *Dancing With the Stars*, Trump deletes that tweet and replaces it with this anodyne dipshittery: "A great try by @seanspicer. We are all proud of you!"

From the Desk of Aldous J. Pennyfarthing
To: Donald Trump, ballot box poison

Dear Pr*sident Assclown,

Dude, you can't get a GOP governor reelected in *Kentucky*, of all places. How the fuck do you think you're going to get a cloddish banana slug through to the next round of *Dancing With the Stars*?

Yes, in the latest demonstration of your *merde*-ass touch, your former press secretary Sean Spicer went down in flames on *Dancing With the Stars* after you wholeheartedly endorsed him on Twitter.

And then you deleted that tweet after he lost. Because telling people to vote for a guy on a reality show who later loses is apparently too embarrassing for you to handle. (And yet you leave the house every day looking like a bowl of processed cheese grits.) I assume that tweet will end up in the same ultra-secure server where you buried the transcript of your July 25 call with Volodymyr Zelensky.

I mean, you really shouldn't take Spicer's defeat personally, Li'l Donny. I've seen him dance before. He looks like a frog trying to escape from a bucket. No one would even think twice about it if you weren't such a weirdo about guarding your reputation as an influencer.

Then again, Republican governors and members of Congress are dropping like flies lately, and you appear to be the bug zapper at the center of it all.

Hey, maybe Sean Spicer's loss is just another grim harbinger of what's to come in 2020.

We can dream, anyway.

Love,
Pennyfarthing

November 12, 2019

- Trump tweets, "Many of the people in DACA, no longer very young, are far from 'angels.' Some are very tough, hardened criminals. President Obama said he had no legal right to sign order, but would anyway. If Supreme Court remedies with overturn, a deal will be made with Dems for them to stay!"
- In a speech at the Economic Club of New York, Trump claims his daughter Ivanka has created 14 million jobs as part of her White House role. Approximately 6 million jobs have been created since Trump's inauguration.

November 13, 2019

- On the first day of public impeachment hearings, the House Intelligence Committee hears testimony from top diplomat William Taylor and Deputy Assistant Secretary of State George Kent. Taylor testifies that a staffer told him he overheard a call between Trump and Gordon Sondland about "the investigations": "Following that meeting, in the presence of my staff at a restaurant, Ambassador Sondland called President Trump and told him of his meetings in Kiev. The member of my staff could hear President Trump on the phone asking Ambassador Sondland about 'the investigations.' Ambassador Sondland told President Trump that the Ukrainians were ready to move forward. Following the call with President Trump, the member of my staff asked Ambassador Sondland what

> President Trump thought about Ukraine. Ambassador Sondland responded that President Trump cares more about the investigations of Biden, which Giuliani was pressing for."

From the Desk of Aldous J. Pennyfarthing
To: Donald Trump, scofflaw

Dear Pr*sident Assclown,

Happy Public Impeachment Hearings Day!

I'll let Adam Schiff field this one.

From his opening statement:

> "The facts in the present inquiry are not seriously contested. Beginning in January of this year, the President's personal attorney, Rudy Giuliani, pressed Ukrainian authorities to investigate Burisma, the country's largest natural gas producer, and the Bidens, since Vice President Joe Biden was seen as a strong potential challenger to Trump.
>
> "Giuliani also promoted a debunked conspiracy that it was Ukraine, not Russia, that hacked the 2016 election. The nation's intelligence agencies have stated unequivocally that it was Russia, not Ukraine, that interfered in our election. But Giuliani believed this conspiracy theory — referred to as 'Crowdstrike,' shorthand for the company that discovered the Russian hack — would aid his client's reelection.
>
> "Giuliani also conducted a smear campaign against the U.S. ambassador to Ukraine, Marie Yovanovitch. On April 29, a senior State Department official told her that although she had 'done nothing wrong,' President Trump had 'lost confidence in her.' With the sidelining of Yovanovich, the stage was set for

the establishment of an irregular channel in which Giuliani and later others, including Gordon Sondland — an influential donor to the president's inauguration now serving as ambassador to the European Union — could advance the president's personal and political interests.

"Yovanovich's replacement in Kyiv, Ambassador Bill Taylor, is a West Point graduate and Vietnam veteran. As he began to better understand the scheme through the summer of 2019, he pushed back, informing Deputy Assistant Secretary Kent and others about a plan to condition U.S. government actions and funding on the performance of political favors by the Ukrainian government — favors intended for President Trump that would undermine our security and our elections.

"Several key events in this scheme took place in the month of July. On July 10th, Ambassador Sondland informed a group of U.S. and Ukrainian officials meeting at the White House that, according to Chief of Staff Mick Mulvaney, a White House meeting desperately sought by the Ukrainian president with Trump would happen only if Ukraine undertook an investigation into 'the energy sector,' which was understood to mean Burisma and, specifically, the Bidens. National Security Advisor Bolton abruptly ended the meeting and said afterwards that he would not be — quote — 'part of whatever drug deal Sondland and Mulvaney are cooking up on this' — end quote.

"A week later, on July 18, a representative from OMB, the White House agency that oversees federal spending, announced on a video conference call that Mulvaney, at the direction of the president, was freezing nearly $400 million in security assistance authorized and appropriated by Congress and which the entirety of the U.S. national security establishment supported.

"One week after that, Donald Trump would have the now-infamous July 25th phone call with Ukrainian President Zelensky. During that call, Trump complained that the U.S. relationship with Ukraine had not been 'reciprocal.' Later, Zelensky thanks Trump for his support 'in the area of defense,' and says that Ukraine was ready to purchase more Javelins, an anti-tank weapon that was among the most important deterrents of further Russian military action. Trump's immediate response: 'I would like you to do us a favor, though.'

"Trump then requested that Zelensky investigate the discredited 2016 'Crowdstrike' conspiracy theory, and even more ominously, look into the Bidens. Neither of these investigations were in the U.S. national interest, and neither was part of the official preparatory material for the call. Both, however, were in Donald Trump's personal interest, and in the interests of his 2020 reelection campaign. And the Ukrainian president knew about both in advance — because Sondland and others had been pressing Ukraine for weeks about investigations into the 2016 election, Burisma and the Bidens.

"After the call, multiple individuals were concerned enough to report it to the National Security Council's top lawyer. The White House would then take the extraordinary step of moving the call record to a highly classified server exclusively reserved for the most sensitive intelligence matters.
"In the following weeks, Ambassador Taylor learned

new facts about a scheme that even Sondland would describe as becoming more insidious. Taylor texted Sondland, 'Are we now saying that security assistance and WH meeting are conditioned on investigations?'

"As summer turned to fall '[i]t kept getting more insidious,' Mr. Sondland testified. Mr. Taylor, who took notes of his conversations, said the ambassador told him in a September 1 phone call that 'everything was dependent' on the public announcement of investigations 'including security assistance.' President Trump wanted Mr. Zelensky 'in a public box.' 'President Trump is a businessman,' Sondland said later. 'When a businessman is about to sign a check to someone who owes him something, the businessman asks that person to pay up before signing the check.'

"In a sworn declaration after Taylor's testimony, Sondland would admit to telling the Ukrainians at a September 1st meeting in Warsaw 'that resumption of U.S. aid would likely not occur until Ukraine provided the public anti-corruption statement that we had been discussing for many weeks.'

"The president's chief of staff confirmed Trump's efforts to coerce Ukraine by withholding aid. When Mick Mulvaney was asked publicly about it, his answer was breathtaking: 'We do that all the time with foreign policy ... I have news for everybody: get over it. There's going to be political influence in foreign policy. That is going to happen.' The video of that confession is plain for all to see.

"Some have argued in the President's defense that the aid was ultimately released. That is true. But only after Congress began an investigation; only after the president's lawyers learned of a whistleblower complaint; and only after members of Congress began asking uncomfortable questions about quid pro quos. A scheme to condition official acts or taxpayer funding to obtain a personal political benefit does not become less odious because it is discovered before it is fully consummated. In fact, the security assistance had been delayed so long, it would take another act of Congress to ensure that it would still go out. And that Oval Office meeting that Zelensky desperately sought — it still hasn't happened.

"Although we have learned a great deal about these events in the last several weeks, there are still missing pieces. The president has instructed the State Department and other agencies to ignore congressional subpoenas for documents. He has instructed witnesses to defy subpoenas and refuse to appear. And he has suggested that those who do expose wrongdoing should be treated like traitors and spies.

"These actions will force Congress to consider, as it did with President Nixon, whether Trump's obstruction of the constitutional duties of Congress constitute additional grounds for impeachment. If the president can simply refuse all oversight, particularly in the context of an impeachment proceeding, the balance of power between our two branches of government will be irrevocably altered. That is not what the Founders intended. And the prospects for further corruption and abuse of power, in this administration or another, will be exponentially increased.

"This is what we believe the testimony will show — both as to the president's conduct and as to his obstruction of Congress. The issue that we confront is the one posed by the president's acting chief of staff when he challenged Americans to 'get over it.' If we find that the president of the United States abused his power and invited foreign interference in our elections, or if he sought to condition, coerce, extort, or bribe an ally into conducting investigations to aid his reelection campaign and did so by withholding official acts — a White House meeting or hundreds of millions of dollars of needed military aid — must we simply 'get over it'? Is that what Americans should now expect from their president? If this is not impeachable conduct, what is? Does the oath of office itself — requiring that our laws be faithfully executed, that our president defend a constitution that balances the powers of its branches, setting ambition against ambition so that we become no monarchy — still have meaning?

"These are the questions we must ask and answer. Without rancor, if we can, without delay regardless, and without party favor or prejudice if we are true to our responsibilities. Benjamin Franklin was asked what kind of a country America was to become. 'A republic,' he answered, 'if you can keep it.' The fundamental issue raised by the impeachment inquiry into Donald J. Trump is: Can we keep it?"

Yeah, I realize that's way too long for you to actually read, so here's a quick summary: "Eat a dick, Chachi. Sooner or later, you're going down."

Love,
Pennyfarthing

◆ ◆ ◆

November 15, 2019

- Trump confidant Roger Stone is convicted on seven counts, including making false statements and witness tampering.
- *The Washington Post* reports that Trump's Doral resort was added as a finalist to host the 2020 G7 summit at the 11th hour after the original list of 10 potential sites had been whittled down to four.
- David Holmes, a top aide to William Taylor, testifies in the House impeachment probe. In his opening statement, he appears to confirm that there was a quid pro quo between Trump and Ukrainian President Zelensky: "I heard President Trump then clarify that Ambassador Sondland was in Ukraine. Ambassador Sondland replied, yes, he was in Ukraine, and went on to state that President Zelensky 'loves your ass.' I then heard President Trump ask, 'So, he's gonna do the investigation?' Ambassador Sondland replied that 'he's gonna do it,' adding that President Zelensky will do 'anything you ask him to.'"
- As former U.S. ambassador to Ukraine Marie Yovanovitch testifies in the Trump impeachment hearing, Trump tweets, "Everywhere Marie Yovanovitch went turned bad. She started off in Somalia, how did that go? Then fast forward to Ukraine, where the new Ukrainian President spoke unfavorably about her in my second phone call with him. It is a U.S. President's absolute right to appoint ambassadors. They call it 'serving at the pleasure of the President.' The U.S. now has a very strong and powerful foreign policy, much different than proceeding [sic] administrations. It is called, quite simply, America First! With all of that, however, I have done FAR more for Ukraine than O."

From the Desk of Aldous J. Pennyfarthing
To: Donald Trump, the masque of the orange death

Dear Pr*sident Assclown,

Yes, as everyone knows, nothing happens in a war-torn Third World country without the say-so of all newly hired 20-something low-level diplomats. Yovanovitch should be ashamed of herself. Lettin' all those warlords do all that warlordin'.

And why did she let the 1984 Somalia famine happen after arriving there in 1986? What the fuck was she thinking?

So here was *The New York Times*' fact-check of your effervescently vile, callow, and moronic tweet:

> There's no credence to the notion that countries "turned bad" when Yovanovitch went to them.
>
> "I don't think I have such powers, not in Mogadishu and Somalia and not in other places," she said when asked about Trump's tweet.
>
> Of the seven countries where Yovanovitch served U.S. interests, five were designated hardship posts. In that sense, they were "bad" to begin with.
>
> Mogadishu, Somalia, was her first tour after she joined the foreign service in 1986. She was a general-services officer with little clout, before she moved to other countries in increasingly senior positions.

You really need to Google *post hoc ergo propter hoc* ("after this, therefore because of this"). It's a classic logical fallacy that means you can't blame Donald Trump every time an Olive Garden bathroom is declared a federal Superfund site no matter how recently he's used it.

Also, as Yovanovitch was testifying, Adam Schiff read your dumbass tweet to her and asked how she felt about it: "It's very intimidating," she said.

So let's just add witness intimidation to your articles of impeachment, umkay, Swifty?

I mean, even the Fox News gooberheads were saying your tweet showed poor judgment. And they praise you every time you appear in public without your scrotum stuck in your zipper.

This is bad for you, dude. Really, really, *really* bad. And a lot more witnesses are queued up.

Enjoy that.

Love,
Pennyfarthing

❖ ❖ ❖

November 16, 2019

- Trump tweets, "Dow hits 28,000 - FIRST TIME EVER, HIGHEST EVER! Gee, Pelosi & Schitt [sic] have a good idea, 'lets Impeach the President.' If something like that ever happened, it would lead to the biggest FALL in Market History. It's called a Depression, not a Recession! So much for 401-K's & Jobs!"
- Mark Sandy, the deputy associate director for national security programs at the Office of Management and Budget, testifies in the House impeachment probe. He says the decision to freeze aid to Ukraine was irregular and that senior members at the OMB were unable to give an explanation for the delay.

❖ ❖ ❖

November 17, 2019

- Trump makes an unscheduled visit to Walter Reed

- Medical Center. The White House says he went to the hospital to undergo a portion of his annual physical, but the unusual nature of the visit prompts speculation that he was there due to a medical emergency of some kind.
- Trump tweets, "Tell Jennifer Williams, whoever that is, to read BOTH transcripts of the presidential calls, & see the just released ststement [sic] from Ukraine. Then she should meet with the other Never Trumpers, who I don't know & mostly never even heard of, & work out a better presidential attack!"
- Republican Eddie Rispone, whom Trump campaigned heavily for, loses his challenge against Louisiana Gov. John Bel Edwards.
- After North Korea calls Joe Biden a "rabid dog" who should be "beaten to death," Trump tweets, "Mr. Chairman, Joe Biden may be Sleepy and Very Slow, but he is not a 'rabid dog.' He is actually somewhat better than that, but I am the only one who can get you where you have to be. You should act quickly, get the deal done. See you soon!"

November 18, 2019

- Following Trump's tweet urging Kim Jong Un to "act quickly" to get a deal done, North Korean Foreign Ministry adviser Kim Kye Gwan states, "I interpreted President Trump's tweet on the 17th to signify a new DPRK-US summit" but "we are no longer interested in these meetings that are useless to us."
- An ABC poll reveals that 70 percent of Americans think Trump's decision to ask Ukraine to investigate Joe Biden and his son was wrong.
- Trump tweets, "Our Crazy, Do Nothing (where's

USMCA, infrastructure, lower drug pricing & much more?) Speaker of the House, Nervous Nancy Pelosi, who is petrified by her Radical Left knowing she will soon be gone (they & Fake News Media are her BOSS), suggested on Sunday's DEFACE THE NATION that I testify about the phony Impeachment Witch Hunt. She also said I could do it in writing. Even though I did nothing wrong, and don't like giving credibility to this No Due Process Hoax, I like the idea & will, in order to get Congress focused again, strongly consider it!"

From the Desk of Aldous J. Pennyfarthing
To: Donald Trump, whooooooooooooooo!

Dear Pr*sident Assclown,

Fuck YAAAAAAAAAAA!

Show those snowflakes what you're made of, Mr. President!

This is why I love you, man! You *strongly consider* defending yourself under oath! Can't wait till you *seriously contemplate* testifying IN FUCKING WRITING or VIA A FUCKING PROXY! Oh, yeah. Nervous Nancy 'bout to get smacked in the face with a big ol' truth dookie!

When this is over, how about you and me grab a couple of cases of Busch Light, snort meth until our faces look like King Tut's taint, and whip old people's Meals on Wheels crullers at gay war refugees?! The *ridged* ones! Those fucking sting, man. Believe me, I know.

It would be EPIC, dude!

You are the KING! In that you literally think you're ABOVE THE LAW! Fuck yaaaaaaaaaa!

I can't believe how triggered Nervous Nancy and Shifty Schiff and all these other fucking libtards get by you.

Hey, what the fuck is on this Starbucks cup? THAT AIN'T NO BABY JESUS! FUUUUUUUUUUUUCCCCCCCCKKKKKKK!

Love,
Pennyfarthing

November 19, 2019

- Lt. Col. Alexander Vindman, Jennifer Williams, Tim Morrison, and Kurt Volker testify in the public impeachment hearings. Volker dismisses accusations against Joe Biden, stating, "At the one in-person meeting I had with Mayor Giuliani on July 19, Mayor Giuliani raised, and I rejected, the conspiracy theory that Vice President Biden would have been influenced in his duties as vice president by money paid to his son. As I testified previously, I have known Vice President Biden for 24 years. He is an honorable man and I hold him in the highest regard."

November 20, 2019

- While touring a plant that makes Apple computers, Trump says, "We're seeing the beginning of a very powerful and important plant. And anybody that followed my campaign, I would always talk about Apple — that I want to see Apple building plants in the United States. And that's what's happening." Later, while criticizing the impeachment hearings, he says, "We're opening up massive Apple plants." He also tweets, "Today I opened a major Apple Manufacturing plant in Texas that will bring high paying jobs back to America. Today Nancy Pelosi closed Congress because she doesn't care about American Workers!" The plant has been making Apple computers since 2013, it's not an Apple plant, and Congress was in session as usual. According to a CNN fact check, this was the third time in 2019 that Trump falsely took credit for opening a plant he had toured.

- In his opening statement in the House impeachment inquiry, U.S. ambassador to the EU Gordon Sondland says, "[A]s I testified previously, Mr. Giuliani's requests were a quid pro quo for arranging a White House visit for President Zelensky. Mr. Giuliani demanded that Ukraine make a public statement announcing investigations of the 2016 election/DNC server and Burisma. Mr. Giuliani was expressing the desires of the president of the United States, and we knew that these investigations were important to the president. ... [I]n July and August 2019, we learned that the White House had also suspended security aid to Ukraine. I was adamantly opposed to any suspension of aid, as the Ukrainians needed those funds to fight against Russian aggression. I tried diligently to ask why the aid was suspended, but I never received a clear answer. In the absence of any credible explanation for the suspension of aid, I later came to believe that the resumption of security aid would not occur until there was a public statement from Ukraine committing to the investigations of the 2016 election and Burisma, as Mr. Giuliani had demanded." Sondland also says, "Everyone was in the loop."

- Presumably in response to the day's impeachment testimony, Trump tweets, "If this were a prizefight, they'd stop it!" He also claims Gordon Sondland's testimony exonerates him because Sondland had repeated Trump's own statement about wanting nothing from Ukraine.

From the Desk of Aldous J. Pennyfarthing
To: Donald Trump, Cray-Doh Dung Factory

Dear Pr*sident Assclown,

Question: Is the Adderall in your alternate universe spiked with psilocybin? Because that tweet doesn't reflect anything that I've seen today.

I swear, we're about two days away from you showing up at the Lincoln Memorial in the middle of the night with Kleenex boxes on your feet.

Dude, this could not be any clearer:

> "[A]s I testified previously, Mr. Giuliani's requests were a quid pro quo for arranging a White House visit for President Zelensky. Mr. Giuliani demanded that Ukraine make a public statement announcing investigations of the 2016 election/DNC server and Burisma. Mr. Giuliani was expressing the desires of the president of the United States, and we knew that these investigations were important to the president."

That's pretty much the whole ball of wax right there. Claiming today was a win for you is like saying the Deepwater Horizon spill was all about free oily shrimp for underprivileged kids.

And, you know, some people manage to get through life without ever *once* taking credit for the opening of a factory they had nothing to do with. How do you do it three times in one year?

At this point you might as well open your next press conference by telling everyone you're the Green Lantern. What's the difference between that and what you're already doing? Sack up, dude. Go for it. No more dicking around. Bet the farm on one big lie. Let's see how it goes.

Love,
Pennyfarthing

❖ ❖ ❖

November 21, 2019

- Fiona Hill and David Holmes testify in the House impeachment hearings. Hill, a former top Russia adviser for the Trump administration, rebukes Republicans for advancing the idea that Ukraine had interfered in the 2016 election: "Based on questions and statements I have heard, some of you on this committee appear to believe that Russia and its security services did not conduct a campaign against our country — and that perhaps, somehow, for some reason, Ukraine did. This is a fictional narrative that has been perpetrated and propagated by the Russian security services themselves."
- In response to David Holmes' assertion that he overheard an incriminating cellphone conversation between Trump and Gordon Sondland in which Trump asked about Ukraine's willingness to investigate the Bidens, Trump, who sounds like a pair of mating Yukon moose being sucked into a jet engine, tweets, "I have been watching people making phone calls my entire life. My hearing is, and has been, great. Never have I been watching a person making a call, which was not on speakerphone, and been able to hear or understand a conversation. I've even tried, but to no avail. Try it live!"

❖ ❖ ❖

November 22, 2019

- Trump conducts a rambling, 53-minute phone interview with Fox & Friends. During the interview, he doubles down on the long-debunked Crowdstrike-Ukraine conspiracy theory. He also appears to admit that he held up aid to Ukraine in order to force the investigations he wanted: "I mean, I asked it very point-blank because we're looking for corruption. There's tremendous corruption. ... Why should we be giving hundreds of millions of dollars to countries when there's this kind of corruption?"

November 24, 2019

- After clashing with Trump over the military's decision to discipline Navy SEAL Eddie Gallagher after Gallagher posed for a photo with a dead ISIS fighter, Navy Secretary Richard Spencer is asked to resign. In his resignation letter, Spencer writes, "In regards to the key principle of good order and discipline, I cannot in good conscience obey an order that I believe violates the sacred oath I took in the presence of my family, my flag and my faith to support and defend the Constitution of the United States."
- *The Washington Post* reports that a review of Trump's decision to withhold aid from Ukraine revealed documents that showed "an after-the-fact justification for the decision and a debate over whether the delay was legal, according to three people familiar with the records."
- In an interview with Fox News, outgoing Energy Secretary Rick Perry calls Trump "the chosen one" and says he was sent by God to rule over America.

November 25, 2019

- While signing the Women's Suffrage Centennial Coin Act, Trump says, "I'm curious why wasn't it done a long time ago, and also — well, I guess the answer to that is because now I'm president. We get things done. We get a lot of things done that nobody else got done." Why had no previous president signed an act commemorating the 100th anniversary of women's suffrage? We'll let you figure that one out all on your own. And since you're not Donald Trump, it should be easy.
- *The Washington Post* reports that Trump has put Jared Kushner in charge of getting his southern border wall built. According to *The Post*, "One person involved in the construction of the wall, who spoke on the condition of anonymity to talk candidly, said Kushner has annoyed officials involved in the process because they said he displayed a lack of knowledge about the government procurement process and the 'realities' of the project."

November 26, 2019

- During a rally in Florida, Trump claims liberals are trying to rename Thanksgiving.
- During his Florida rally, Trump tries to debunk imaginary mainstream media claims that he had recently suffered a heart attack, saying, "They said, he went into the hospital — and it's true, I didn't wear a tie — why would I wear a tie if the first thing they do is say take off your shirt, sir, and show us that gorgeous chest? Show — we want to see, sir. We've never seen a chest quite like it." ABC news later reports,

> "Despite his claim that it had been reported that his 'tremendous pain' was a heart attack, ABC News could not find any major news media reporting that he had experienced such a condition and the White House physician Dr. Sean Conley has denied Trump had chest pain."

From the Desk of Aldous J. Pennyfarthing
To: Donald Trump, tremendous pain

Dear Pr*sident Assclown,

"Show us that gorgeous chest"?

Yeah, I'm pretty sure they said "engorged."

Though I *do* believe that they said, "We've never seen a chest quite like it." That part definitely rings true.

Granted, I've never seen your chest — and believe me, I don't want to. I imagine even *glancing* at those fulsomely titian man-tits would be like staring into the eyes of Satan ... or a basilisk ... or Gary Busey. I'd either go mad or turn to stone.

Also, *no* major media outlets claimed you'd had a heart attack. Some people were speculating about what you were really in the hospital for, since the White House is basically just a 24/7 lie factory now. But that's on you, Chesty LaRue.

To wit: No one is trying to rename Thanksgiving. But that didn't stop you from pulling this outlandish lie out of your dingleberry-larded Donald Trump:

> "As we gather for Thanksgiving, you know, some people want to change the name Thanksgiving. They don't want to use the term Thanksgiving. ... People have different ideas why it shouldn't be called Thanksgiving, but everybody in this room, I know, loves the name Thanksgiving. And we're not changing."

Oh, yay! Crisis solved! You're a miracle worker! Maybe now you can do something about the liberal crusade to dub sex with barnyard animals "Trump-humpin'." But be quick about it. It's taking off faster than our War on Thanksgiving. You know what we liberals are like.

Love,
Pennyfarthing

November 27, 2019

- Trump tweets out a doctored photo of his head on Rocky Balboa's body.

November 28, 2019

- CNN reports that the Trump administration has decided to "substantially" cut its contribution to NATO's collective budget.
- Trump visits the troops in Afghanistan and brags about himself.

November 29, 2019

- Trump's talk of a cease-fire with the Taliban takes the Afghanis by surprise. According to *The Washington Post*, "[N]either the Taliban nor the government of Afghan President Ashraf Ghani indicated that a cease-fire was near, or even being discussed in resumed U.S. negotiations."

◆ ◆ ◆

December 1, 2019

From the Desk of Aldous J. Pennyfarthing
To: Donald Trump, Christmas yam

Dear Pr*sident Assclown,

My publisher says I need to get this book released in time for the holiday shopping season, so this will be the final missive of this magnum opus.

I realize I've been harsh. Granted, it's for your own good, but it does make me feel a bit queasy sometimes. You're only human, after all — and I'm a good person, really, despite the tsunami of vitriol straining the delicate spine (or e-spine, as it were) of this slim chronicle of fucknuttery.

So please indulge me as I bid adieu with an excerpt from Charles Dickens' *A Christmas Carol*. It's one of my favorite passages from that timeless, beloved work and could well serve as a keynote for this joyous season of gemütlichkeit and goodwill. It's from a soliloquy by Scrooge's nephew to his mean and miserly Uncle Ebenezer.

> "But I am sure I have always thought of Christmas time, when it has come round — apart from the veneration due to its sacred name and origin, if anything belonging to it can be apart from that — as a good time; a kind, forgiving, charitable, pleasant time: the only time I know of, in the long calendar of the year, when men and women seem by one consent to open their shut-up hearts freely, and to think of people below them as if they really were fellow-passengers to the grave, and not another race of creatures bound on other journeys. And therefore, uncle, though it has

never put a scrap of gold or silver in my pocket, I believe that it has done me good, and will do me good; and I say, God bless it! Oh, also — fuck you, you scabrous, mushroom-crotched, ocher-faced, butterball-looking halfwit bridge troll in a zesty, piquant orangutan-diaper-and-Christmas-plum pudding."

So, yeah, merry Christmas. And thank you for making it okay to say "fuck you, Mr. President" again. 'Tis the season, as they say.

Love (and happy holidays),
Pennyfarthing

❖ ❖ ❖

Note to my fellow warriors in the Trump resistance: I enjoy writing these books, and I sincerely hope you enjoy reading them. That said, as I noted in the introduction, I *really* hope this is the penultimate volume. I desperately want the title of the next book in this series to be *Goodbye, Asshole*. The cover is already designed and ready to go. It's awesome; you'll love it. Please don't make me wait another five years to unveil it.

Assuming dummy's ass isn't tossed out of office before the November elections, I'll plan on launching the next book mere days (or even hours) after we elect a new president.

But my (and presumably your) dream won't come true unless we all do our part. Please, support Trump's opponent no matter who it is. No purity tests, no waiting around for inspiration. It's all hands on deck.

We simply can't let this racist oaf clodhop around the Oval Office for another half-decade. Our country's future — not to mention our collective mental well-being — depends on *you*.

Make it so.

Get involved. Get out the vote. Be a patriot.

Thank you.

Pennyfarthing out.

Made in the USA
Coppell, TX
12 April 2020